W9-BLI-550

The current values in this book should be used only as a guide. They are not intended to set prices, which vary from one section of the country to another. Auction prices as well as dealer prices vary greatly and are affected by condition as well as demand. Neither the Authors nor the Publisher assumes responsibility for any losses that might be incurred as a result of consulting this guide.

Searching for a Publisher?

We are always looking for knowledgeable people considered to be experts within their fields. If you feel that there is a real need for a book on your collectible subject and have a large comprehensive collection, contact us.

COLLECTOR BOOKS
P.O. Box 3009
Paducah, Kentucky 42002-3009

Cover design: Beth Summers
Book design: Pamela Shumaker

On cover: top left - Celluloid child on metal sleigh, $50.00 - 65.00; bottom left - 1920's Fold-out, $120.00 - 140.00; middle - Snowman candy container, $50.00 - 70.00; top right - 3" figure light, dog, $60.00 - 95.00; bottom right - peacock ornament, 1920's - 50's, $25.00 - 30.00.

Additional copies of this book may be ordered from:

Collector Books
P.O. Box 3009
Paducah, KY 42002-3009

Margaret and Kenn Whitmyer
P.O. Box 30806
Gahanna, OH 43203

@$24.95 Add $2.00 for postage and handling

Copyright: Margaret and Kenn Whitmyer, 1994

This book or any part thereof may not be reproduced without the written consent of the Authors and Publisher.

Dedication

To Ziggy, Pat, and Ian – Collector, Advocator, Future Collector

Acknowledgments

We wish to thank our many friends — collectors, dealers, and associates — who have worked very hard to make this book a reality. These people have donated their time to give us advice and have tracked down elusive items for photography. They have invited us into their homes to photograph their collections and have made suggestions for pricing. All this generosity is deeply appreciated.

Friends who deserve special recognition for outstanding contributions include Bruce Knight, Mike Girard, Bob and Diane Kubicki, Dave and Ricki Chennault, and Jackie and Ray Stockwell. All their efforts are deeply appreciated.

Perhaps the person who worked the hardest was our photographer, Seigfried Kurz. He took well over 700 pictures and had the additional responsibility of having them printed properly. He also is a collector of Christmas ornaments. His knowledge and contacts with other collectors in this field made our job much easier.

Other persons to whom we are deeply indebted include:

Miles Bausch	Doug Lucas
Joyce and Parke Bloyer	Nancy Maben
Rita & John Ebner	Gene Massie
Mary Lou Esterline	Fred McMorrow
Bridget Fugate	Ruth Overly
Audrey & Joseph Humphrey	Bill & Debbie Reese
Shari Knight	Bunny Walker
Clarence Loose	

Finally, the staff of CPI Photofinishing at Eastland Mall in Columbus deserves to be commended for having the patience and taking the time to produce the quality prints we desired. We realize we demanded more than their average customer, and thank them for making an extra effort.

Contents

Christmas – The Celebration

Christmas is an annual festival held in the Christian church to celebrate the birth of Christ. The exact origin of this celebration is unknown. However, over the centuries both Christian and pagan elements have conbined to produce the celebration as we know it today.

Among historians, the birth of Christ is thought to have occurred approximately 2,000 years ago. However, the actual day of His birth has been placed in practically every month of the year by one scholar or another, and no one has ever proven that December 25th is the birthday of Christ. As a matter of fact, Biblical evidence suggests He may have been born in the late summer or early fall.

Why was this date chosen, and by whom was it selected? If this time in history is taken into consideration, it should probably be safe to assume that the primary influence on Christian celebrations would be the culture of the Roman Empire. Later as the empire crumbled and missionaries spread the Christian message throughout Europe, customs and traditions of the barbarians would blend with and alter the Roman celebrations.

The early Romans had several festivals which occurred about December 25th. One was Saturnalia, honoring Saturnus, the god of seeds and growing. This was a week of wild parties, games, and revelry which lasted from December 17th to the 24th. All businesses were closed. This was a time of total joy in honor of a god who ruled when all men were happy and good. Presents were exchanged among men of all classes. One popular present was the candle. These probably symbolized the recurrence of the sun's power which at that time of the year was just beginning to re-emerge after the winter solstice. A mock king was chosen, and he presided with absolute authority over the festivities.

Another Roman celebration, even wilder than Saturnalia, was just a few days later. On January 1st the celebration of the New Year began. This was a three day festival called Kalends during which houses were decorated with greenery and candles. Presents called strenae were given to children, friends, and the poor. During this festival men dressed up in animal hides and in women's clothes. They donned masks and paraded through the streets; perhaps they were the forerunners of our mummers.

Before their conversion to Christianity in the third century, the Romans had established a holiday on December 25th. Emperor Aurelian, who was a follower of Mithraism, established that date as the festival of Dies Invicti Solis (the Day of the Invincible Sun). Mithraism was embraced by the Romans until the conversion of Constantine to Christianity in 336 A.D. The Romans loved to celebrate. These new converts saw no reason why they could not substitute the celebration of the birth of their Son of Righteousness for their previous celebration honoring the rebirth of the earthly sun. A few years later in 350 A.D., Pope Julius acknowledged December 25th as the official day for the celebration of the birth of Christ.

After the conversion of Rome, missionaries began to wander into the other pagan areas of Europe. These areas were inhabited by barbarians whose primary concerns were food, shelter, and other materialistic things. Therefore, they engaged instinctively in ceremonies which revolved around the essentials of earthly life. They paid tribute to the gods of nature to insure themselves a better life on earth. The missionaries taught these people that their current life was not important. They should give up their celebrations and magical rites and look forward to their spiritual life.

The church fought an increasingly futile battle against man's instinct for earthly satisfaction. Toward the end of the sixth century, Pope Gregory began the process of blending wilder pagan customs into the stricter Christian celebrations of the birth of Christ. This liberalization continued to occur until a peak was reached in about the fifteenth century. Shortly therafter, the forces of the Reformation threw Europe into turmoil. Man became more sophisticated and the scope of the festivals came under closer scrutiny. Serious Protestants viewed the wild celebrations as merely an excuse to continue the customs of Saturnalia. They viewed these ideas as pagan and preferred a more serious and quiet celebration.

In 1647 when the Puritans and Cromwell came to power in England, Christmas was abolished as a legal holiday and punishments were established for its observance. Riots resulted, but the Puritans persisted, and any outward pagan-like celebration was restricted. After the monarchy was restored again in 1660, the celebration of Christmas was resumed, but the revitalized holiday observance lost much of its old culture, and has never completely recovered from this devastating blow.

American celebration of Christmas has been strongly influenced by the homeland of each area's immigrants. New England felt the Puritan influence much longer than England did. In many parts of the Puritan-settled northeast there was a ban on the observance of Christmas until after the Civil War. Other immigrants such as the Dutch in New York and the German and Irish settlers celebrated Christmas in much the same manner as they had done previously in their native lands. Gradually, the customs of the various nationalities became intertwined, and the celebration of Christmas across the country became more uniform.

Slowly, Christmas began to be recognized as a legal holiday in the United States. Alabama was the first state to proclaim December 25th a legal holiday in 1836. Slowly other states followed, and in 1890 Christmas became a legal holiday in this country.

The following pages explore various customs associated with the celebration of Christmas, such as the legend of St. Nicholas, the symbolism of the tree and its decorations, and many of the legends that have evolved through the years.

St. Nicholas – Father Christmas – Kriss Kringle
Santa Claus

Our modern Santa Claus is a composite figure, drawn from the history, legends, and folklore of many countries. He evolved from a Saint, was demoted to an evil gnome, and finally became the jolly, robust character children know and love today. Santa Claus has survived both religious and political persecution. His legend is alive, well, and growing.

The custom of giving gifts has been with us for centuries. The early Romans were known to exchange gifts during the festivals of Saturnalus and Kalends. Many of these pagan customs were later assimilated into Christian practices and eventually central characters who represented and were part of the gift-giving ritual began to emerge.

The first of these symbolic figures was St. Nicholas, a Bishop of Myra in Asia Minor during the fourth century A.D. This bishop was very generous to the poor and was kind and gentle to the children. Very little is actually known about the life of St. Nicholas; however, historians think he participated in the First Council of Nicaea in 325 A.D.

He only became a legend after his death and was adopted as the patron saint of children. Over the years this saint has been adopted by sailors, bankers, pawnbrokers, and even thieves. The day of his death, December 6, has long been celebrated as St. Nicholas Day. For centuries, children were visited on that night by a gift-bearing old man with a long white beard who rode on a white horse and answered to the name St. Nicholas.

St. Nicholas and all other Catholic bishops became very unpopular among the Protestants during the Reformation in the sixteenth century. However, the tradition of gift-giving and the idea of a central figure to bear the gifts had been firmly established by this time. Therefore, a simple name change for this central character was all that was necessary to preserve the tradition. St. Nicholas became Weihnactsmann (Christmas man) in Germany, Father Christmas in England, and Pere Noel in France.

Besides a change in name, this split within the church also brought about other changes in the tradition of Father Christmas. More of the pagan elements were added to the legend. He was often represented as a combination of the pagan gods Thor and Saturn. Thor was a Norse god, represented by an old man with a beard, who roared through the heavens battling the gods of ice and snow to help his people endure the treacherous northern cold, and Saturn was the Roman god who provided food, wine, joy, and equality to all people. Father Christmas also developed a split personality; he could either reward or punish. Companions, who were sometimes sinister, often helped Father Christmas on his annual journey.

In northern Germany St. Nicholas' alter ego became Knecht Rupprecht. He often appeared clad in straw or skins, and his job was to reward the good and cause the guilty to repent. He later became known as Ru-Klas or rough Nicholas because of his rugged appearance.

In other parts of Germany, the Christ Child (Christkindchen) became the gift-giver on Christmas Eve. The Christ Child was an angellic type figure, who wore a white robe and white jewelled crown, had golden wings, and rode a mule. Entry to a child's house was made through the keyhole. The Christkindchen was accompanied on his journey by Pelze Nicol, a boy with a beard and a blackened face. The good children were rewarded with sweets by this Pelze Nicol, and the mothers of the bad children received switches, so these children would be reminded of their evil deeds. When the German immigrants came to America, they brought this legend with them. Here the name of the Christ Child changed to "Kriss Krindle" and finally to "Kriss Kringle." This child bearing gifts finally evolved into the old man who is synonymous with our Santa Claus. The Pennsylvania Dutch immigrants also brought Pelze Nicol with them to America. Here the pronunciation was soon transformed to pelsnickle. Then with further deterioration it became belschnickle or belsnickle. Today, we call these sinister-looking representations of St. Nicholas belsnickles.

Meanwhile, the Dutch continued to have visits from St. Nicholas. Dutch immigrants in the New York area brought the influence of St. Nicholas to the United States in the 1600's. The pronunciation of "St. Nicholas" gradually deteriorated to "Sinte Claes." By the end of the Civil War the sound had evolved to its present day "Santa Claus."

The modern legend of Santa Claus had its beginning with Washington Irving in his book Diedrich Knickerbocker's *A History of New York form the Beginning of the World to the End of the Dutch Dynasty*. In this popular book St. Nicholas was established as a patron saint for the Dutch, and he was given magical powers which enabled him to fly over rooftops in his horse and wagon.

In 1822 Clement C. Moore added to the legend in his poem "An Account of a Visit of St. Nicholas." On December 23, 1823, this poem appeared anonymously in *The Troy Sentinel* of Troy, New York. (Although it received an immediate enthusiastic response, it was several years before Clement Moore acknowledged his role as author.) In this poem Santa Claus was described as having a sleigh and reindeer, and the annual trip down the chimney was popularized.

During the late 1800's the appearance of Santa Claus began to change. The drawings of Thomas Nast were largely responsible for this transformation. In his pen and ink drawings for *Harper's Weekly* Santa changed from a stern-appearing thin old man to a jolly, roly-poly, elf-like character. In 1897 eight-year old Virginia O'Hanlon, upon being told by some of her friends there was no Santa Claus, asked wishfully in her letter to the *New York Sun* if there was indeed a Santa Claus. The following reply by Francis P. Church, editor of the Sun, firmly established the spirit of Santa Claus in the hearts of children everywhere.

Virginia, your little friends are wrong. They have been affected by the skepticism of a skeptical age. They do not believe except they see. They think that nothing can be which is not comprehensible in their little minds. All minds, Virginia, whether they be men's or children's are little. In this great universe of ours man is a mere insect, an ant in his intellect as compared with the boundless world about him, as measured by the intelligence capable of grasping the whole of truth and knowledge.

Yes, Virginia, there is a Santa Claus. He exists as certainly as love and generosity and devotion exist, and you know that they abound and give to your life its highest beauty and joy. Alas! How dreary would be the world if there were no Santa Claus! It would be as dreary as if there were no Virginias. There would be no childlike faith then, no poetry, no romance to make tolerable this existence. We should have no enjoyment, except in sense and sight. The eternal light with which childhood fills the world would be extinguished.

Not believe in Santa Claus! You might as well not believe in fairies! You might get your papa to hire men to watch all the chimneys on Christmas Eve to catch Santa Claus, but even if they did see him coming down, what would that prove? Nobody sees Santa Claus, but that is no sign there is no Santa Claus. The most real things in the world are those that neither children nor men can see. Did you ever see fairies dancing on the lawn? Of course not, but that's no proof that they are not there. Nobody can conceive or imagine all the wonders that are unseen and unseeable in the world.

You may tear apart the baby's rattle and see what makes the noise inside, but there is a veil covering the unseen world which not the strongest man, nor even the united strength of all the strongest men that ever lived, could tear apart. Only faith, fancy, poetry, love, romance, can push aside that curtain and view and picture the supernal beauty and glory beyond. Is it all real? Ah, Virginia, in all this world there is nothing else real and abiding.

No Santa Claus! Thank God! He lives, and he lives forever. A thousand years from now he will continue to make glad the hearts of childhood.

This reply was probably a little complicated for the mind of an eight-year-old, but it firmly expounded the belief in Santa Claus. How could anyone disbelieve and shatter the hopes of innocent childhood?

In the late 1800's life-like images of Santa Claus also began to appear frequently on postcards. By the 1920's and 1930's Santa Claus began to assume an important role in the Christmas advertising campaigns of certain companies. He appeared in robust human form in the ads of such companies as Coca-Cola, Cream of Wheat, Whitman Chocolate, Interwoven, and others. During the past 50 years the appearance of Santa Claus has changed very little. Perhaps the biggest change has been in the manner in which Santa Claus has been incorporated in the commercialization of Christmas. His jolly robust figure is heavily counted on to jingle the cash registers of many businesses.

In the following pages the change in the appearance of Santa Claus over the last 100 years will be apparent. The variety of figures shown ranges from some of the oldest and most expensive to some of the newest and least expensive. Whether he is old or new, by whatever name he is known — St. Nicholas, Father Christmas, Kriss Kringle or Santa Claus — he is a symbol of Christmas sought by collectors everywhere.

Plate 1. These two papier-mache belsnickles are from the late 1800's. The one on the left is wearing a hooded, red-trimmed coat which is covered with mica. He is of German origin and stands 12" high. The belsnickle on the right is wearing a white hooded, mica-covered coat. It is 11" high. Notice the detail of the molding and the thinner shape of this belsnickle. These are characteristics of the early figures and increase their desirability. Both of these figures still have their original feather trees with red composition berry tips.

Plate 2. These similar papier-mache belsnickles are wearing white, mica-covered, hooded coats. They were made in Germany and are carrying green goose feather branches. Both are 8½" high. Belsnickles with white robes are among the most easily found, although none of the larger ones are common.

Plate 3. Both these early belsnickles are wearing green, hooded, mica-coated coats. The one on the left is 10" high, and the one on the right is 8" high. They are made of plaster-coated papier-mache and were produced in Germany around 1900. Belsnickles with green coats are not easy to find.

Plate 4. These three medium-size papier-mache belsnickles were made in Germany during the early 1900's. The one with the red coat is 9½" high. The one in the center with a rare blue coat is 8½" high, and the one with the white mica-covered coat is 8" high. Originally, all three sported green feather trees.

Plate 6. This example of a molded cardboard Father Christmas is attributed to Germany after WWI. The front and back halves of the figure are stapled together to form the complete piece. He is 9" high.

Plate 5. These two German papier-mache belsnickles are 6" and 7" high. Their feather trees are not original and should be much smaller. The one on the left is wearing an unusual green coat. The additional red trim around the hood makes this figure even more desirable.

Plate 8. The red belsnickle on the left with the open flap in his robe is very unusual. He is missing his legs and is now only 6" high. The jolly appearing Roly-Poly Santa is a 9" high composition design offered by Schoenhut in the early 1900's. The Santa with the red coat, blue trousers, and cane is a Japanese figure from the mid-1930's. This Santa is 6" high and has a clay face. The red belsnickle on the right is a German papier-mache figure from the early 1900's. This figure is 9" high and should have a feather tree inserted into the hole in his arm.

Plate 7. The belsnickle in this photo has a blue coat adorned with a lot of mica. He is holding a small goose feather branch with a red berry tip. The bottom of this 9" high candy container is marked "Made in Germany."

Plate 9. This stooped representation of a pre-1900 German Father Christmas is complete with a three branch goose feather tree with red berries. His clothes and toy bag are felt. His face is papier-mache, and the beard is made of rabbit fur. Notice the trace of snow on his robe. At 11" high, he is unusually large for a figure of this type.

Plate 10. This papier-mache Father Christmas figure was made in Germany in the late 1880's. He is wearing a long snow-covered felt robe. His original rabbit fur beard has been replaced, and he is missing the sled he was pulling. He is 7½" high.

Plate 11. These two old Father Christmas figures are both candy containers. Both have rabbit fur beards, are of German origin, and were made about the turn of the century. They have plaster over papier-mache faces and hands. Both are wearing brown cotton flannel robes. The stern belsnickle-type faces of these figures are typical of many of the early German Father Christmas representations. The early miniature toys they are carrying are seldom found. The figure on the left is 11" high, and the one on the right is 10" high.

Plate 12. This turn of the century Father Christmas candy container is 14½" high. His hands and face are made of plaster, and his beard and eyebrows are fashioned from rabbit fur. He is wearing a mica encrusted, fur-trimmed, and red felt coat and hat. His right hand is clutching a bundle of switches.

Plate 13. The clock-works nodder Father Christmas figure featured here is 30" high. He has a composition face, a rabbit fur beard, and a long red felt robe. His companion, a 14" tall child, is clutching a basket which is decorated with feather tree sprigs.

Plate 14. The Father Christmas bust pictured here stands 18" high and is a Newell Post decoration. He has a composition face, a rabbit fur beard, and a felt coat and cap adorned with mica.

Plate 15. Father Christmas is bringing some lucky child a teddy bear. He is 22" high and has a composition face with a rabbit fur beard. His red cotton flannel coat and hat are trimmed in white.

Plate 16. This rather jovial-looking Father Christmas is from Germany and was given as a Christmas present in 1912. His suit is cotton flannel. He has a rabbit fur beard and stands 10" tall. His trousers are blue bloomers, and he is carrying a large goose-feather tree.

Plate 17. The two Father Christmas figures shown here are early 1900's clock-works nodders. The face, head, and feet of each is made of papier-mache. Both are clothed in full-length flannel robes tied with rope belts. Each is carrying a goose feather tree and presents. Notice the smaller figure has a more pleasant facial expression than was common during this time period. They are of German manufacture and have the typical rabbit's fur hair and beard which is characteristic of these figures. The figure on the left is 29" high, and the one on the right is 40" high.

Plate 18. This clock-works nodder is in excellent condition and works beautifully. The long red felt robe is nicely accented with white trim. Father Christmas is complete with a rope belt and an attached woven basket. He is 26" high and was made in the early 1900's.

Plate 19. This German Father Christmas is a turn of the century clock-works nodder. When wound the head of this Santa nods up and down much like the pendulum of a clock swings back and forth. His feet, face, and hands are papier-mache. He is dressed in a long flannel robe with a white rope belt. He stands 28" high, and his beard and hair are rabbit fur.

Plate 20. This bespectacled Father Christmas mantle sitter is a clock-works nodder. The glasses are gold filled, and his suit is wool. The head and feet are made of papier-mache, and he stands 16" high.

Plate 21. The stick-mount on the Santa on the left may not be original, but it has been this way for a long time. The figure is cotton with a cotton robe and a plaster face. The Santa figure is 4½" high, and the entire piece is 10" long. The figure on the right is a papier-mach candy container which is 6½" high. His beard is made of rabbit fur, and his robe is made of felt. He has a ribbon belt and was made during the early 1900's.

Plate 22. The papier-mache candy container to the right is 8" high. He has a cotton flannel suit and a rabbit fur beard. He was made in Germany about 1920.

Plate 23. The German figure in this photo is 6" high and is riding in a wooden 12" long sled. The Santa has a rabbit fur beard and a long cotton flannel robe which is secured by a rope belt. His face and hands are papier-mache, and his legs are wire.

Plate 24. This late nineteenth century hand-carved wooden puppet is fully jointed and exhibits the craftsmanship of the era. His hand sewn flannel suit is original, but his beard and hair appear to have been replaced. He is also carrying a bottle brush tree which is from a much later date. The puppet stands 18" high.

Plate 25. Notice the mask face on the straw-filled satin-clothed Santa on the left. This American Santa from the early 1920's has a cotton beard and is wearing composition boots. He has mittens for hands and is 26" high. The figure on the right is a jointed composition doll from the early 1930's. His beard and hat are molded composition, and his suit is cotton. He is 16" high.

Plate 26. This compostion Santa doll is very similar to the one in Plate 25 on the right. His facial expression is slightly different. He is carrying a toy bag and has a black leather belt as the other one probably had at one time. This figure has tall, straight black boots while the other one is wearing flared galoshes which are topped with white trim. He stands 19" high.

Plate 27. This papier-mache Santa looks as if he is on the verge of having a bright idea. He is from the early 1940's and is marked "UNGER'S FIBER PRODUCT CELL-U-PON UNGER DOLL AND TOY COMPANY, MILWAUKEE, WISCONSIN."

Plate 28. The Santa figure pictured here dates to the 1940's. It was used as a store display for the Lazarus department stores of Columbus, OH. He is 31" high and has a composition face, felt clothes and bag, and a rabbit fur beard. This is a mechanical figure with moveable head and arms.

Plate 29. This German, papier-mache, Father Christmas candy container figure dates from the 1920's. He has a cotton beard, stands 18" high, and is carrying a feather tree adorned with pine cones. The lighted base and cute friend were provided by a thoughtful owner during the twenties.

Plate 30. The Santa on the left is Japanese and dates from the 1930's. He has a cotton suit and composition face, hands, and boots. He is 14" high. The skinny figure on the right is German and probably dates to the early 1920's. He is 10" high, has composition hands and face, and is wearing a cotton flannel suit.

Plate 31. This colorful 1930's Japanese Santa has a very fierce-looking face. His face and hands are compostion. He is wearing a fake fur-trimmed cotton flannel suit, which has a paper belt and buckle. He is 9" high and is marked "MADE IN JAPAN. DISTRIBUTOR CALIENT FOR BEAUTY, INC., BSYN, ILL."

Plate 32. The figure on the left is a typical Japanese candy container Santa. He is 7" high and has a cotton-flannel suit, clay face, and a mesh bag for candy. The large 10" high Japanese Santa in the middle has a maribou-trimmed, cotton-flannel suit. He has a clay face with large blue eyes and a fluffy cotton beard. The Japanese figure on the right is 7½" high. He has a red cotton-flannel coat and blue bloomers. All these Santa figures are from the 1930's.

Plate 33. The Santa on the left holding the lamb is Japanese and is from the 1930's. He has a clay face and cotton flannel suit and is missing his white cardboard base. The figure in the center is Japanese and has bendable wire legs. He has a papier-mache face and hands, a cotton beard, and a cotton flannel suit. He is 7½" high. The Santa on the right is German. He has a clay face and cotton flannel robe and is standing on a white cardboard base. He is 5½" high.

Plate 34. The skiing Santa on the left was made in Occupied Japan. He is made of cotton, has a plaster face, and is 3¾" high. The Japanese figure in the center is 6½" high. He is cotton with a plaster face and hands. The earlier belsnickle type figure on the right is also from Japan. He has a wicked-looking papier-mache face with a rabbit fur beard. His pants are made of fur, and his coat is cotton flannel. He is 5" high.

Plate 35. This Japanese Santa from the early 1930's is enjoying his ride in his gilded cardboard sled. The figure is cotton with a plaster face and is only 2½" high. The papier-mache reindeer and cardboard sled are 7" long.

Plate 36. The sleigh on the left is Japanese. It is 9" long. The other two sleighs and Santa figures were made in Germany. The larger sleigh is 6½" long, and the Santa is 4" high. The small sleigh is 4" long, and the Santa is 2½" high.

Plate 37. Santa Claus is enjoying a ride in his sleigh. The coated cardboard sleigh is covered with mica. It is being pulled by two celluloid reindeer. The Japanese Santa is 4" high, and the entire set is 11" long by 2" wide.

Plate 38. The two Santa figures on the left are cotton with plaster faces and were made in Japan during the 1930's. The figure to the left is sitting in a cardboard sleigh which is being pulled by a cotton reindeer. The entire piece is 5" long. The Santa in the center is in a sitting position and is 3" high. The figure on the right is a German pre-1920 papier-mache Santa. He has a rabbit fur beard and a cotton flannel coat with a rope belt. He is carrying a goose feather tree and is 5" high.

Plate 39. The Santa on the left is 9" high and bears the mark "Western Germany." He has a plaster face, cotton beard and a wool robe. He is from the late 1940's. The figure on the right is Japanese and has a clay face. He is 6" high and is from the 1930's.

Plate 40. The figures in this photo were all made in Japan. The Santa on the left in the gold-colored, mica coated, cardboard sled is 3¼" high. The second Santa from the left is 4½" high. He has a plastic face and a tubular cardboard body. He is wearing a red cotton coat and dark blue cardboard trousers. A paper label on the bottom reads "Japan 5c." The large Santa in the center is 6" high. He has a papier-mache face, wire arms, a tubular cardboard body, blue cotton felt trousers, and a red cotton felt coat. The Santa on the skis is 3½" high. He has a tubular cardboard body, wire arms, blue cotton bloomers, a red cotton felt coat, and black cardboard boots.

Plate 41. All three of these figures are Japanese. The one on the left is 5¼" high and is marked "Made in Occupied Japan." He has a papier-mache face, clay hands and feet, and is wearing a paper imitation felt coat. The Santa figure in the center is 9" high. He has wire arms with cotton hands, clay legs and feet, and a papier-mache face with a fluffy cotton beard. He is wearing a white-trimmed red cotton suit and is carrying a green cotton bag. The Santa on the right is 6" high and is marked "Made in Occupied Japan." He has a cardboard torso which is covered with purple satin and red cotton clothing. His hands and face are made of clay, and he is carrying a bright green bag.

Plate 42. The two figures in this photo are marked "Made in Japan." The Santa on skis is 5½" high. He has a papier-mache face and a tubular cardboard body. He is wearing a red cotton felt coat and blue cotton trousers. He is supported by skis which are 7" long. The Santa on the right is 7½" high. He has a plastic face, cotton beard, wire arms, and clay legs and feet. He is holding a red berry-tipped, gold colored vinyl branch in his right hand. His left arm is clutching a rope which is attached to the large brown bag he is carrying on his back.

20

Plate 43. Pictured in this photo are two 9" high Japanese cotton batting Santa ornaments. They have papier-mache faces and cotton bodies and appendages. Shape is maintained by using wire to preserve the body form.

Plate 44. Father Christmas appears to be waving at the children. His body, face, and beard are papier-mache. His suit is red flannel with white flannel trim. He is holding a goose feather tree with red composition berries. Of German origin he dates from the early 1900's and stands 12½" high.

Plate 45. A variety of molded cardboard Santa figures were made. This one is an American made candy cane holder from the late 1940's. It stands 10" high.

Plate 46. This large papier-mache Santa head is 18" high. It is nicely detailed, and its appearance is enhanced by the addition of gold glitter. Many of these heads were used in department store displays.

Plate 47. This later papier-mache Santa has white boots and a black top hat. He was moded very crudely, and no attempt was made to give him a distinguishable belt. He is 11" high.

Plate 48. This stuffed doll appears quite fierce with his straggly rabbit fur beard and hair. He has a celluloid face, satin suit, and felt hat. He is 18" high and probably dates from the early 1930's.

Plate 49. Notice the shredded beard on this satin-suited Santa doll from the 1930's. He has a very jolly appearance and came complete with bells on his fancy shoes. He has a cloth face and is 20" high.

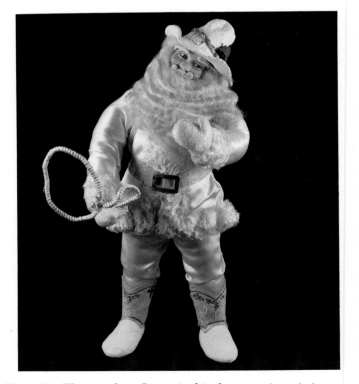

Plate 50. This cowboy Santa in his fancy satin suit is very unusual. He is a product of the 1940's, has a plastic face, and is 26" high.

Plate 51. This happy Santa with the white satin suit with fake fur trim is 28" high. He has a plastic face and a very bushy cotton beard.

Plate 52. The original version of this toy Santa and sleigh was made in the early 1900's. The piece pictured here is from a 1920's reproduction. Both versions are collectible, but the older one sells for a much higher price. Notice the small wheels on the 16" long sleigh are missing.

Plate 53. Mechanical cast iron banks are very desirable. The original model of this bank was made in the United States by J.E. Stevens in the late 1800's. Later versions have "Santa Claus" embossed on the base and have been made at various times from the 1930's to the present.

Plate 54. Small cast iron Father Christmas figures are sometimes found in the form of banks. This bank is from the early 1900's and is 6" high.

Plate 55. The metal Santa on skis is 2¼" high. Note the back of the skis are missing. The reindeer is pot metal and was made in Germany. It is 2½" high.

Plate 56. This tin wind-up walking Santa was made by Chein from the late 1920's and into the 1930's. This colorful little Santa is 5½" high.

Plate 57. Pictured here is a battery powered tin Santa which turns the pages of the book at which he is looking. He is 7½" high, has a cotton beard, and is wearing a cotton suit.

Plate 58. Pictured here is a 6½" high Santa with his arms extended. A wind-up mechanism causes his arms to move up and down. It also produces an internal shaker movement which causes the Santa to dance around. He has a papier-mache face and is wearing a cotton felt robe.

Plate 59. The figure on the left is a tin wind-up toy. The reindeer is tin and walks when the key is wound. He is 5½" long and 5½" high. The Santa on the sled is wearing a chenille suit. He is being pulled in his sled by a papier-mache reindeer.

Plate 60. This battery powered Santa drummer is from the 1950's. He was made in Japan and sold in America by the Cragston Corporation of New York. He has a plastic face and a tin body and is wearing a red cotton-flannel suit.

Plate 61. The battery powered Santa drummer is 9½" high. He has a plastic face, a red cotton felt coat, and a long white cotton beard. He is marked "Trademark ALPS Made in Japan." The bell-ringing Santa is also powered by batteries. He is seated atop a house which doubles as a bank. The mark, "HTC Japan" is on the side of the house. The figure is 11½" high.

Plate 62. The large Santa on the left is battery operated and stands 13" high. When he is operating, he rings his bells, and his eyes light. He is Japanese and was made during the early 1950's. The Santa in the middle is key wound and is 10" high. He has a celluloid face and rings his bell when wound. The small Santa on the right is key wound, stands 5½" high, and has a celluloid face. This Santa marches and swings his arms when wound.

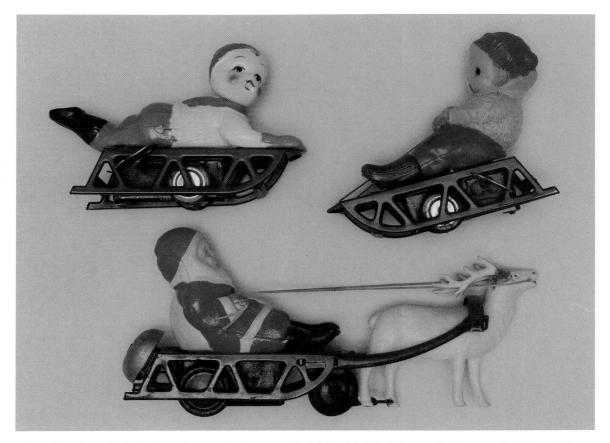

Plate 63. The celluloid Santa is on a 7" long metal sleigh which is being pulled by a celluloid reindeer. The bell on the rear of the sleigh rings when the wheels turn. The celluloid children on the metal sleds are wind-up toys. Both examples are marked "Made in Occupied Japan" and are 5" long.

Plate 64. The celluloid Santa figures in this photo are all marked "Irwin, Made in U.S.A." The Santa on skis is 4" high, the one in the center is 5" high, and the one on the right is 4" high.

Plate 65. The celluloid Santa on the left is 3½" high. He is standing on a large white base and is holding a white cane in his right hand. The figure in the center with the red boots is 4¾" high. He is marked "Japan." Traces of the original red are all that remain on the suit of the Santa on the right with the black boots. He is 7½" high and is marked "Japan."

Plate 66. All of these celluloid Santa figures were made in Japan. The two on the ends are waving with their right hands. The one on the left is 4¼" high, and the one on the right is 6¼" high. Notice the jointed legs on the figure in the center. He is 5" high.

Plate 67. The celluloid Santa figures in this photo are holding baskets of fruit. They are about 5" high and have no identifying marks.

Plate 68. "Made in U.S.A." is the trademark of all these celluloid figures. The two smaller figures are 7" high, and the Santa in the center is 8½" high. This larger Santa was made by Irwin.

Plate 69. The figures in this picture are all made of celluloid. The small Santa on the left is 4" high and is marked "Irwin, Made in U.S.A." The Santa on the motorcycle was made in Japan. He is 4" high, and the motorcycle is 5" long. The figure on the right is 4" high. This is a jolly Santa who is hiding a small doll behind his back.

Plate 70. These three celluloid figures are typical of the many which were produced. The Santa on the left is 5" high. The small Santa is only 1½" high. These were sometimes used as package decorations. The Santa on the sleigh is 4¾" long.

Plate 71. Displayed in this picture are some very colorful celluloid figures. The two small figures are 4" long, and the Santa in the middle is 9" high. This type of figure was made in the United States, Germany, and Japan from the late 1920's until the early 1940's.

Plate 72. The plastic Santa in this picture is riding a colorful tin motorcycle. This wind-up toy is marked "Made in Japan." It is 3" high and 3½" long.

Plate 73. This celluloid Santa is waving from his 10" long sleigh.

Plate 75. The two decorative items in this photo are made of celluloid. Both of these sleighs are being pulled by two reindeer. The figure at the top is 5¼" long, is marked "Made in Occupied Japan," and has its reindeer side by side. The piece at the bottom is 10½" long, has bells on the harness, and has two reindeer with one behind the other.

Plate 74. The decorative items featured here include small to medium-size celluloid Santa figures in sleighs. The red and white sleigh at the top left is 4½" long. Toys are piled in front of Santa, and the sleigh is marked "Made in U.S.A." The decoration at the top right features a toy-laden sleigh which is being pulled by a large white reindeer. This piece is 4½" long. The sleigh and reindeer combination at the bottom left is 3½" long. It is marked "Irwin Toys, U.S.A." The large red sleigh at the lower right is 6½" long and is marked "Japan."

Plate 76. All three of these small decorative pieces are celluloid candy containers. The two sleighs are 3¼" long, and the car is 3½" long.

Plate 77. These celluloid cars and trucks are laden with toys and feature Santa as the driver. Top left: White truck with a green tree, 3¼" long; Top right: Red truck marked "Japan," 3¾" long; Center: Red and white truck with green tree marked "Irwin Toys U.S.A." 3¼" long; Bottom left: White car marked "Japan," 4" long; Bottom right: Red truck marked "Japan," 4¼" long.

Plate 78. This decoration is 10½" long. The Santa and reindeer are celluloid, and the sleigh is cardboard.

Plate 79. This old wooden cut-out Santa is 11" tall. He is nicely decorated and merrily ringing his bell. Currently, many of this type of wooden cut-outs are being made.

Plate 80. A bakery in Pittsburg, PA used this wooden sleigh as a window decoration in the early 1920's. It is over 6' long and saw many years of service.

Plate 81. The figure on the left is a troll bank. This representation of Santa is a plastic figure, 8½" high, with a cotton beard and cotton-flannel suit. Trolls were originally made in Sweden. Later, they were produced in the U.S.A. A similar, but slightly different, doll is being made today. The Santa on the right is a plastic figure that is a combination bank and music box. He is 12" high.

Plate 82. This Santa in the unusual white satin suit is 11½" high. He is seated in a wooden sleigh which is 12" long. His face is vinyl, and he has a shredded white satin beard.

Plate 83. Steiff figures are collectible, and these reindeer and Santa are no exception. Although some Steiff Christmas items are still available, these are from the 1950's. The large reindeer are 10" long, and the small reindeer is 6" long. The Santa has a cloth face and is 8½" high. These figures were made in West Germany.

Plate 84. This plaster mantle-sitter Santa is 7½" high. He was made as a craft by a Youngstown, OH lady during the 1950's.

Plate 85. This cute, colorful chalk Santa bank is 11" high. Although he is not very old or expensive, he is an interesting addition to any collection.

Plate 86. The two Santa figures in this picture are plaster banks. The bank with the large green toy bag is 12½" high. It is marked "Copr. L. Mori, 1949."

Plate 87. This colorful Santa decoration is a 7" high ceramic figure. It dates to the 1960's.

Plate 88. This spring-head ceramic Santa figure is 8" high.

Plate 89. This plaster-of-paris Santa head is illuminated with cone-shaped Mazda lamps. The head is 19" in diameter and is an attractive outdoor decoration for any collector's home.

Plate 90. The Santa head shown here is 26" high and 18" wide. It is made of plaster-of-paris and is nicely decorated with holly.

Plate 91. Ceramic decorations from Japan were popular during the 1960's. Left: Santa riding on a sleigh, marked "Napco, Japan," 6" long by 5" high; Center: Santa carrying a large bag, marked "Japan," 6½" high; Right: Santa waving with a large bag on his back, marked "ENESCO, Japan," 6½" high.

Plate 92. The two Coca-Cola Santa figures pictured here are from the 1960's. They are 17" high and have cotton bodies and a plastic face, hands, and boots. The black figure is more desirable than the white one. However, fewer white figures are available, so both colors are priced about the same.

Plate 93. These two rubber Santas are both American made. The one on the left is 11½" high and has a squeaker in his back. He was made by the Rempel Mfg. Co., Inc., Akron, OH. The rubber Santa on the right also has a squeaker and is 8½" tall. This one was made by Sanitoy, Inc., New York.

Plate 94. This unusual looking Santa was made in Czechoslovakia. He is 7¼" high and is carrying a bottle brush tree. His robe is made of red cotton felt, and it is secured with a white rope belt.

Plate 95. This black Santa has a stuffed body, a velvet suit, and a rubber head. He is 13" high. His original box is marked "Knickerbocker Toy Co. Inc., New York, #900/5 Santa."

Plate 96. The figure on the left is an interesting newer Santa Claus. He is plastic with a cotton suit and a very bushy cotton beard. He is 15½" high. The plastic Santa on the right is 17" high and has a hole in his back into which a light bulb may be inserted to produce a lamp.

Plate 97. These two relatively new Japanese Santa figures have cardboard bodies, plastic faces, and cotton suits. The one on the left is 13" high, and the one on the right is 11" high.

The Christmas Tree Story

Long before there was a Christmas, pagans used the evergreen as a symbol. Early man gathered greenery and worshipped evergreens during the long, dark days of winter. They believed these trees possessed magical powers, and if they kept them through the winter, green would return to the forest again in the spring. By the time Christianity reached these areas of northern Europe in the fourteenth century, this pagan ideology was firmly established. The Roman Catholic church found it was much easier to incorporate the use of evergreens into its celebrations than it was to break the pagan's beliefs in the powers of these trees.

At about the same time missionaries were converting the pagans of northern Europe, "miracle plays" became very popular. Originally these "miracle plays" were performances by actors in celebrations outside the churches on the 24th of December. This was observed as Adam and Eve's day on the Calendar of Saints, and the plays were designed to teach the church congregations about the stories of the Bible. One of the most popular plays was about the story of Adam and Eve and was the "tree of Paradise." Since the plays took place in the middle of the winter when apple trees were barren, the evergreens were used to represent the apple trees. Thus, evergreen trees were often decorated with apples, and the plays certainly must have left a very lasting impression among the early converts who thought these trees which stayed green all winter were magical anyway.

Decoration of trees with items other than apples is known to have taken place in Germany in the early seventeenth century. Candles, cookies, and religious ornaments were among the earliest decorations. In parts of Germany candle-decorated wooden pyramids were used in the celebrations. These pyramids developed in northern Germany and were originally twigs tied together in such a manner that a pyramid structure resulted. Candles, apples, and other edibles were tied to the pyramids. Later, pyramids evolved into true works of art with skilled craftsmen competing for the honor of producing the most elaborate decoration. The practice of placing candles on trees was probably borrowed from this early custom of decorating pyramids.

Another custom which developed in parts of Germany was the hanging of the tree from the ceiling and placing lighted candles on this upside down evergreen. The first printed reference to the Christmas tree is in a forest ordinance from the Alsace area of Germany, dated 1561. It states "no burgher shall have for Christmas more than one bush of more than eight shoes' length." This was a conservation measure taken to pro-tect the forests, since already the custom was becoming popular, and too many trees were being cut. During the next hundred years the custom of decorating the evergreen grew in Germany. The first German Christmas trees were small — usually only large enough to set on a table-top. A reference in a travel book from around 1600 tells about Christmas in Strassburg "where they set up fir trees in the rooms and hang on them roses cut of many colored paper, apples, wafers, gilt sugar, and so on." Slowly, decorating trees was introduced to other areas. The practice of setting up fir trees was known in England by the mid 1700's, but was limited to royalty until Prince Albert popularized the use of the Christmas tree in the early 1840's. However, the widespread use of the tree in England was short-lived. The Puritans soon banned the celebration of Christmas with such pagan symbols. This ban and the shortage of natural trees in England combined to stunt the recovery of the English celebration.

The Christmas tree was probably intoduced to the United States by early German immigrants who brought their customs with them. Early Moravians in Pennsylvania during the 1750's are known to have used wooden pyramids in their traditional Christmas celebration. It is widely speculated that the first actual Christmas trees in America were erected by Hessian soldiers in 1776. The first Christmas tree in the White House was during the administration of Franklin Pierce in the 1850's. However, widespread adoption of the Christmas tree by the American public did not occur until the late 1800's.

Soon with the increasing popularity of Christmas trees, conservationists became concerned about the depletion of the nation's forests. This spurred the development of the artificial tree. By the 1890's their use was encouraged by this nations premier conservationist of the time — Theodore Roosevelt.

The artificial tree was developed in Germany, and the earliest examples were carried to the United States by immigrants. These early trees were made from dyed goose and turkey feathers which were attached to wire branches. The branches were wrapped around a wooden trunk which was set into a painted wooden base. The trunk of the tree was then wrapped with green or brown paper to hide the wires and the simulate tree bark. Many of the trees had branches which were finished on the ends with red composition berries or metal candle clips. These early trees, before 1914, were primarily imported from Germany and came in a variety of sizes — from a few inches long to about six feet in height. The sprigs, which were a few inches long, were designed to be carried by the papier-mache Father Christmas figures which were being made during this time. The medium size trees – up to about four feet in height were mostly used as table-top decorations. The larger trees – from four to six feet in height – were designed to sit on the floor.

World War I interrupted the flow of artificial trees into the United States from Germany. During this period feather trees were produced in the United States. Many of these will be found with a "Made in U.S.A." inscription on the base. After the war Germany again became the primary supplier of feather trees. The largest trees were now about eight feet in height and retailed for about nine dollars.

By the early thirties the makers began to experiment with different colored trees. Blue, white, gold, dark green, and light green trees began to appear.

During the early 1930's another type of artificial tree made its appearance on the market. This tree was made of cellophane and was produced by the Standard Cellophane and Novelty Company. Although this type of tree was never very popular, it was sold for about thirty years. This cellophane was not very durable and not very many undamaged examples can be found today.

During World War II the supply of German trees was stopped once more. American-made feather trees filled the gap once again, but the quality of these trees did not approach those of the Germans. The branches of these trees were farther apart, and the feathers were less dense.

After World War II the sales of feather trees began to decline. However, some feather trees continued to be sold by mail order companies until the early 1950's, and some were once again imported from Germany. These will generally be marked "Made in Western Germany."

Gradually, paper, wire, and cloth trees began to replace the feather tree. The paper trees consisted of wire branches wrapped with crepe paper. They were available in sizes ranging from six inches to over eight feet in height and could be found in green, red, blue, or white. Cloth trees had straight wire branches to which a dark green rayon material was attached. They may be found in sizes ranging from forty inches to seven feet tall.

Early in the 1960's aluminum and spun glass artificial trees became the rage. Many of these trees could be seen in picture widows, illuminated by various colored floodlights.

Reproductions of the early feather trees are now being made. Although these new trees are relatively expensive, some have been appearing at flea markets masquerading as old.

Plate 98. The widely spaced branches on this feather tree are typical of the early German feather trees which were made to closely resemble the real European evergreens. This look appears a bit strange to us since we are used to a fuller look. This tree has a combination of red composition berry tip ends and candle clip branch tips. The tree is secured in a crudely fashioned round wooden base and is 36" high.

Plate 99. The feather tree on the left is marked "MADE IN GERMANY" on the base. This tree is 26" high and has a round wood base and red compostion berry limb tips. The feather tree in .the center is a pale green. It has candle clip branch tips, is 22" high, and has a cone-shaped wood base. The feather tree on the right has branches with candle clip tips. It is 32" high and sits in a round wood base.

Plate 100. The feather tree on the left has a square red decorated wooden base and red compostion berry branch tips and is 38" high. The feather tree on the right has a round white wooden base, candle clip branch tips, and is 37" high. Both trees have widely spaced branches. Trees of this type wholesaled for about $4.00 a dozen in the early 1930's.

Plate 101. The feather tree on the left has a white square base with a red holly decoration. It is 29" high and has a combination of red composition berry tip and candle clip branch tips. The tree on the right is 27" high and has red compostion berry branch tips.

Plate 102. This picture illustrates two white feather trees with red composition berry tipped branches. The tree on the left has widely spaced branches and a round wooden base and is 25" high. The tree on the right is of much better quality. The branches are closely spaced, and the feathers are more dense. This tree is 32" high and is mounted on a square red decorated base. Trees like these were produced in the 1930's.

Plate 103. This green goose-feather tree is of fine quality. The branches are very close together, and the feathers are dense. This is typical of many of the smaller table-top trees. The branches have both original candle clip and red composition berry tips. The square base is finished with white enamel and has a wreath and bells for additional decoration. It stands 26" high.

Plate 104. The small feather tree on the left is 16" tall and was presented as a Christmas present in 1907. The tree is shown here with its original ornaments. The feather tree on the right has both candle clips and red composition berries. It is 19" tall and has a plain round wooden base.

40

Plate 105. The presence of the exhaust tips at the top of these carbon-filament lamps suggest this tree was made before WWI. Any lighted tree from that time period would have to be unusual. The tree is paper wrapped with goose feathers dyed green. It has red composition berries and is 44" high.

Plate 106. Pictured here is a nice quality blue spruce feather tree. It is 6' high, has red composition berries and is set in a decorated square white base. Trees of this type from the early 1930's retailed for about $6.00.

Plate 107. The goose feathers of this tree have been dyed a bluish-purple. This unusual color is very striking but seldom found. The tree is 44" high, and the branches have red composition berry tips.

Plate 108. These are two miniature dark green feather trees. The tree on the left is 11" high, and the one on the right is 6" high. Both trees have branch tips which are nicely finished with red composition berries.

Plate 109. These three miniature trees are made of dyed green feathers. They range in size from 5" to 6½". The tree on the left has large red compostion berry-tipped branches, and the other two have paper flowers on the tips of the branches.

Plate 110. These small trees are 8" high. They have vinyl needles and are decorated with candles and colored miniature bulbs.

Plate 111. This tree is 9" high. It has plastic coated cardboard needles and is decorated with small colored bulbs. It is marked "Made in Japan."

Plate 112. These two examples of holly plants are both from Germany. The plant on the left is 6" high and has red composition berries and coated cloth leaves. The plant on the right is 9½" high and has wrapped wire branches and coated cloth leaves. Notice the unusual real pine cone accent.

Plate 113. This picture illustrates two types of wire trees. The tree on the left is 10½" high and is made of stiff wire similar to the consistency of a bottle brush. The tree on the right is 7½" high and is made of fine tinsel-type wire. It is shown with its original ornaments and candles.

Plate 114. These two music-box trees were decorative items from the late sixties. Both trees have heavy wire branches with vinyl needles. The tree on the left is 13" high, and the one on the right is 19" high.

Plate 115. These five trees are of the style which many collectors refer to as "bottle brush." These snow covered bristle-like trees range from 8½" to about 13" high. The tree on the left is complete with its original pressed cotton ornaments. The tree on the right has large glass bulbs, and the base is marked "HAHN, NYC."

Plate 116. These "bottle brush" trees are examples of the types of trees many people used to decorate model railroad villages. They have snow covered bristles and red bases, are about 5" to 8" high, and may be found in great abundance.

Plate 117. Bubble light trees were very popular during the early 1950's. This tree is 19" high, sits in a plastic base, and has cellophane needles.

Plate 118. This type of tree was produced during the 1950's. It is made of white-tinted vinyl and rests on a wooden base which contains a lamp socket. The bulbs on the tree do not light but are instead illuminated by the bulb which is in the base. The tree is 19" high.

Plate 119. The table-top tree shown here revolves and contains a music box in its base which plays "Jingle Bells." The tree is 23" high and has a paper-wrapped wooden center post and heavy wire branches with cloth needles.

Plate 120. Aluminum trees were very popular during the early 1960's but faded from the scene about as rapidly as they appeared. This tree stands 18" high.

Decorating the Christmas Tree
Glass Ornaments

The small town of Lauscha in Germany was the birthplace of the glass Christmas tree ornament. German glassblowers migrated to Lauscha in about 1600 to escape religious persecution. They established a glass-making center and developed a very prosperous industry in the production of glass toys and pharmaceutical items. Later, a process was developed for making hollow glass beads for milliners and jewelers.

Production of beads eventually became the primary source of income for the area. However, in the mid-1840's the Czechs found a process for making glass beads which were far superior to those of the Lauschans. The bead monopoly of the Lauschans ended, and the destitute glassblowers were forced to return to making toys and other utilitatian glass products. After about ten years of experimentation Dr. Louis Greiner-Schlotfeger finally discovered the Czechs' secret method for coloring beads, and the prospects for Lauschan economic recovery appeared brighter.

As a sideline, many Lauschan glassblowers blew large hollow glass balls called "kugels." These decorative heavy glass balls were sometimes hung from the ceilings and windows for protection from evil spirits. Dr. Greiner-Schlotfeger began to color kugels with his new silver solution, and the demand for these ornaments increased dramatically. Soon, other shapes of hollow heavy glass ornaments were being made. Pinecone, pear-shapes, grape clusters, nuts, and apples were among the first shapes.

In the mid-1870's these colorful decorations came to the attention of the toy merchants in nearby Sonneberg. These agents won the export right and took over the international marketing of glass decorations. Within ten years glass ornaments replaced glass toys as their leading export.

An American, F.W. Woolworth, was largely responsible for the rapid increase in sales of glass ornaments. He reluctantly tested his first ornaments with a twenty-five dollar investment in 1880. They sold so rapidly he placed increasingly larger orders the following years and the nickels and dimes soon amounted to over twenty-five million dollars worth of ornaments. Other American companies followed this lead, and ornaments were soon being sold everwhere. With such outstanding sales taking place in this country, German glassblowers expanded their capacity for making ornaments, and many new shapes appeared in the late 1800's and early 1900's.

The rapid expansion of the industry was temporarily interrupted by World War I. However, no suitable replacement for the German ornaments was developed, and the German glassblowers easily recaptured their market with the return of peace. Millions of German glass ornaments were imported during the 1920's and 1930's until a World War again interrupted the flow.

After World War II Lauscha came under Soviet control. Recovery of the German glass industry was very slow, but a new glass center was established in Neustadt in West Germany. This center along with a revitalized center in East Germany is again producing a small number of hand-blown ornaments.

Plate 121. Large heavy glass kugels are greatly appreciated by collectors. Left: Green, 6" high; Center: Blue, 4" high; Right: Silver, 3" high.

Plate 122. Although most kugels were round and shiny, some were decorated with hot wax or hot glass to produce a textured look like the ornament on left. Left: Red, 4½" high; Center: Red, 3" high; Right: Purple, 3" high.

Plate 123. Some kugel-style ornaments are oval. Early ornaments of this shape are not found as easily as the round ones. Left: Blue, 6" high; Right: Gold, 7" high.

Plate 124. American-made heavy glass ornaments are rarely found. According to some people, this ornament, called a "witch's eye," had mysterious magical powers. Around the turn of the century, this ornament was a symbol of good luck. It is 3½" high.

Plate 125. Japanese imitation kugels may sometimes be found. These ornaments are similar in appearance to the German kugels. However, the glass is much thinner, and their weight is much less than that of the German version.

Plate 126. Heavy glass ornaments shaped like grape clusters are often associated with kugels. These were all made in the early 1900's. Left to right: Blue, 7½" high; Silver, 2¾" high; Blue, 6" high; Blue 4½" high.

Plate 127. American attempts to imitate German figurals often brought crude results. This early copy of German figurals is made of heavy kugel-like quality glass. Circa 1910, 2¼" high.

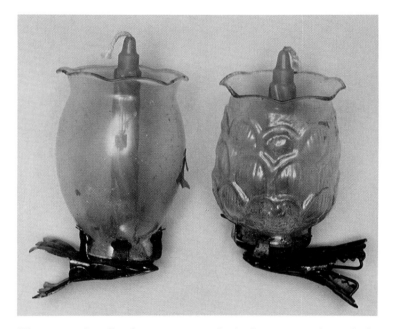

Plate 128. Candle clip ornaments flashed various colors. Only traces of the original color remain on these, 3" high.

Plate 129. Early turn of the century spring clip "Fierce Santa" candle holder. 4" high.

Plate 130. Spring clip ornaments with glass shades were made to hold candles. Circa early 1900's, 3½" high.

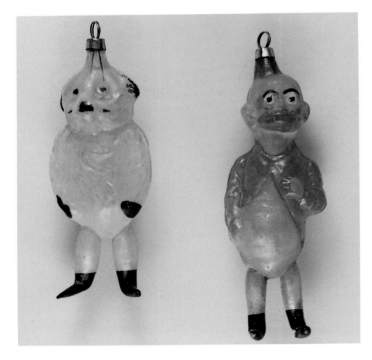

Plate 131. Left: Bear with extended legs, early 1900's, 3" high. Right: Happy Hooligan, early 1900's, 4" high.

Plate 132. Palmer Cox Brownie style figure with extended legs, red jacket, and silver pants, 5" long.

Plate 133. Left: Foxy Grandpa with extended legs, 4½" high.
Right: Keystone Cop with extended legs, 4¾" high.

Plate 134. Foxy Grandpa on a spring clip, 5" high.

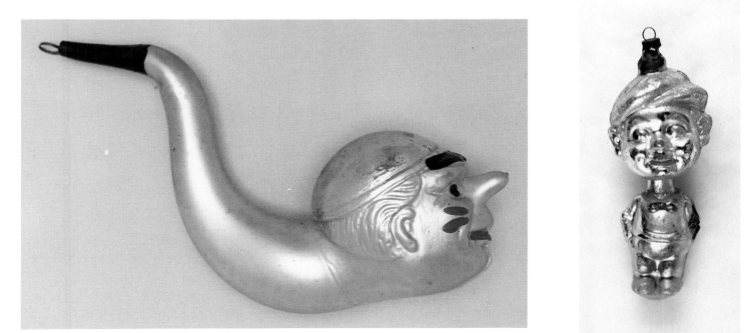

Plate 135. Jockey pipe with a long nose, 5¾" long.

Plate 136. Skeezix, an early
1920's ornament, 4¾" high.

Plate 137. Lady Liberty with real hair. Circa 1920's, 6½" high.

Plate 138. Northwind blowing (also called Man in the Moon), 3¾" long.

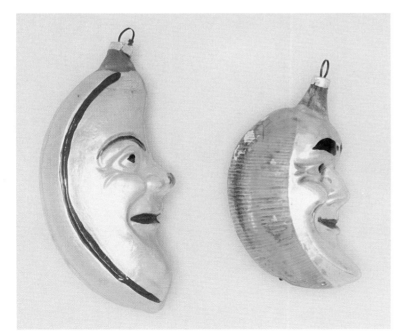

Plate 139. Crescent-shaped Man in the Moon ornaments. Left 4¾", right 3½".

Plate 140. Left: Man on the moon scene, 1920's to 1930's, 2" high. Right: Man playing a mandolin, early 1900's, 6½" long.

Plate 141. Drama face rattle, 4½" long.

Plate 142. Left: Clip-on grape man, 3¾" high. Right: Sour-face grape head, 3½" high.

Plate 143. Left: Grape man, circa early 1900's, 2¼" high. Center: Doll head, relatively new, red cap and painted eyes, 2¼" high. Right: Comical doll face, painted face and eyes, 1¼" high.

Plate 144. Top row: 1. Girl's head with silver hair, 4"; 2. English girl head, 3"; 3. Sailer head on clip, 4". Bottom row: 1. Cherub with blonde hair, 3"; 2. Doll face with blonde hair and blue cap, 3¼".

Plate 145. Left: Old man in pinecone, circa 1930's, 3½". Center: Father Christmas head, 2½". Right: Old man in pinecone, about 1920, 3".

Plate 146. Left: Elf head, 1920's, 2¾". Center: Elf in house, 1920's, 3½". Right: Elf in treehouse, 1920's, 3".

Plate 147. Left: Girl head, glass eyes, circa 1930's, 3". Center: Clown head, circa 1920's, 3½". Right: Clown head, circa 1930's, 3".

Plate 148. Left: Jester head, height, 4½". Center: Clown with banjo, 1930's, 4½". Right: Clown head, 1920's, 3½".

Plate 149. Left: Christ child head, 2½". Center: Girl with golden locks, circa 1920's, 3". Right: Girl in a duster cap, circa 1920's, 2¾".

Plate 150. Left: Cabbage patch-type head, 3¾". Right: Indian bust, 1920's, 3½".

Plate 151. Clockwise from left: 1. Scowling Indian, 3½"; 2. Indian with warpaint, 3½"; 3. Indian with draped bust, 3½"; 4. Indian in a canoe, 4"; 5. Scowling Indian on a clip, 3".

56

Plate 152. Indian head, clip on with candleholder, 4".

Plate 153. Left: Roly-Poly potato head man, 3". Right: Smiling face on a mushroom, 3".

Plate 154. Left: Ringmaster with cardboard hat, 4". Center: Sneering devil's head, 4". Right: Charlie Chaplin, 3¾".

Plate 155. Left: Head of Baby Jesus, 3". Left center: Kite head with spun glass tail, 4½". Right center: Head of girl glancing sideways, 2½". Right: Andy Gump on a clip, 2¾".

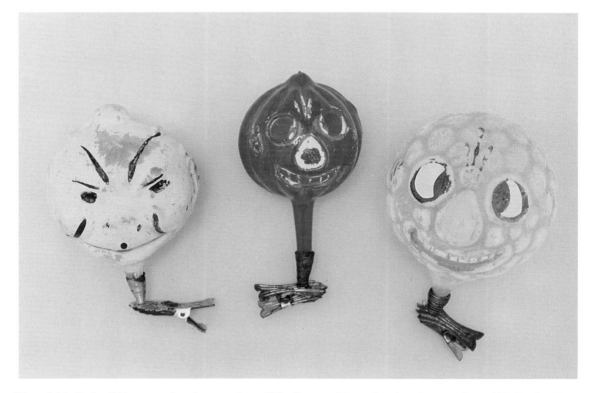

Plate 156. Left: Chinaman head on a clip, 4¾". Center: Pumpkin head on a clip, 4¾". Right: Popcorn head on a clip, 4¾".

Plate 157. Left: Clown head, 3½". Center: Clown head, 3". Right: Clown head, circa 1930's, 3".

Plate 158. Left: Clown with conical body, 6½". Left center top: Embossed juggler, 2¾". Left center bottom: Clown head with ruffled collar, 4". Right center: Pink unsilvered clown on a clip, 4¼". Right: Common shape clown with hands in pockets, 4½".

Plate 159. Left: Coco the Clown, 1920's, 1½". Right: Chubby clown, 1920's, 4".

Plate 160. Common clowns from the 1920's and 1930's. The clown on the bottom right has "My Darling" embossed on his suit. The clown on the top left is American. It is made of very thick glass and is silvered on the outside, 3½" to 4¼" high.

Plate 161. Clown with 500,000 on stomach, early 1900's, 4¼".

Plate 162. Left: Clown on the moon, early 1900's, 3½". Right: Clown with 500,000 on stomach, 1920's, 4¼".

Plate 163. Lady jester with a bell-shaped base, 3¾".

Plate 164. Figure in a jester outfit, 3½".

Plate 165. Punch and Judy, early 1900's, 3".

Plate 166. Hansel and Gretel, 3¾".

Plate 167. Moses in a basket, 3¼".

61

Plate 168. Baby in a bunting, 2¾".

Plate 169. Baby with a pacifier, early 1900's, 2½".

Plate 170. Little boy on sled, early 1900's, 4".

Plate 171. Left: Baby in a blanket, early 1900's, 3¼". Center: Snowbaby, 1920's, 4". Right: Little Miss Muffett, 1920's, 4".

Plate 174. Red Riding Hood, early 1900's, 3".

Plate 172. Swami, sometimes referred to as Aladdin from the Ali Baba tales, 4".

Plate 173. Witch with embossed cat and broom, 4".

Plate 176. Beggar man with mushroom hat, early 1900's, 3½".

Plate 175. Left: Boy with an accordian, 1920's, 3¾". Center: German boy, 1920's, 3½". Right: Goldilocks, 1930's, 3½".

Plate 177. Left: Policeman with a billy club, 4½". Center Hessian soldier, 5¼". Right: Baby aviator, 5".

Plate 179. Left: Patriotic lady, 3". Right: Mrs. Santa Claus, 1920's, 3½" high.

Plate 178. Top left: Butcher or baker, 3¾". Top right: Girl in a flower basket, 3¼". Bottom left: Dutch boy, 4½". Bottom right: Girl with a spoon and carrot, 3¾".

Plate 181. Angel tree top ornaments, 5".

Plate 180. Left: Girl's face in a flower, 2½".
Right: Girl's face in a flower candle clip, 3¾".

Plate 182. Left to right: a. Pinchushion girl, 4¼"; b. girl in a flower clip-on 3½"; c. choir girl, 3½"; d. Kate Greenaway clip-on, 4½"; e. angel with blonde hair, 3½".

Plate 183. Angel with flowers and scrap face, circa 1900, 3½" high.

Plate 184. Clip-on angel with Dresden wings, 4½". Angel on a silver ball, 5".

Plate 185. Left: Snowman on a clip, 3¾". Right: Angel on a clip with Dresden wings, 4".

Plate 186. Left: Snowman, frosted body, 1950's, 3½". Center: Snowman, 1930's, 3½". Right: Snowman, frosted body, 1950's, 3½".

Plate 187. Left: Snowman in a chimney, 4". Center: Snowman on a white ball, 5". Right: Snowman on a ball with a silver net, 4½".

Plate 188. Left: Santa with tree, 1920's to 1930's, 3". Left center: Santa, 1920's to 1930's, 3". Right center: Santa with tree, 1920's to 1930's, 3". Right: Large Santa head with bushy beard, 1950's, 5".

Plate 189. Left: Fierce-looking Santa with a tree, 1920's, 3½". Right: Common Santa with a tree, 1930's, 3".

Plate 190. Left: Santa on ball, 1920's to 1930's, 3¾". Center: Santa with tree 1920's to 1930's, 3¼". Right: Red Santa with green basket, 1920's, 3½".

Plate 191. Left: Santa in chimney, 1930's, 3". Center: Santa in chimney, 1920's, 3½". Right: Santa with tree, 1920's to 1930's, 4½".

Plate 192. Left: Red and silver Santa with silver feet, 3¾". Left center: Santa with red coat and white feather tree, 4¼". Center: Santa on a clip, 3¾". Right center: Santa with gold legs and a gold bag, 3⅜". Right: Santa with a long beard, 5½".

Plate 193. Left: Clip-on Santa with a white coat and scrap face, 4¼". Center: Clip-on Santa with glass eyes, 5". Right: Santa with blue pipe cleaner type legs and black composition boots, 5".

Plate 195. Left: Gold Santa scene, early 1900's, 3½". Right: Silver Santa scene, early 1900's, 3½".

Plate 194. Left : Santa holding tree, 1930's, 3¾".
Right: Santa on clip holding bag, 1920's, 6".

Plate 197. Santa tree top ornament, 4¼".

Plate 196. Left: Santa with basket, 1920's to 1930's, 4". Right: Santa with basket, 1920's to 1930's, 4".

Plate 198. Left: Bell with embossed Santa in a blue robe, 2½". Left center: Santa with a green tree and yellow bag standing on a bell, 3½". Right center: Blue Santa standing on a bell with a scrap angel face, 5". Right: Angel with yellow hair standing on a bell.

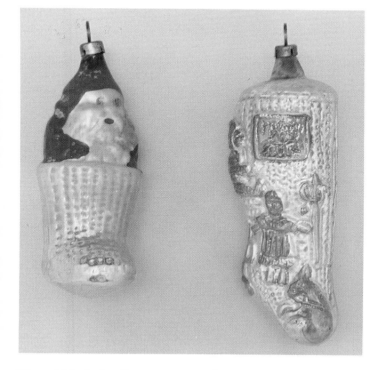

Plate 199. Left: Santa in a stocking, 3½". Right; Green stocking with embossed red children and toys, 4".

Plate 200. Snow white and the Seven Dwarfs, 8-piece set, late 1930's. Snow White, 6"; Dwarf, 5". Copyright 1938 by Walt Disney Enterprises and made by the Paper Novelty Manufacturing Company of New York.

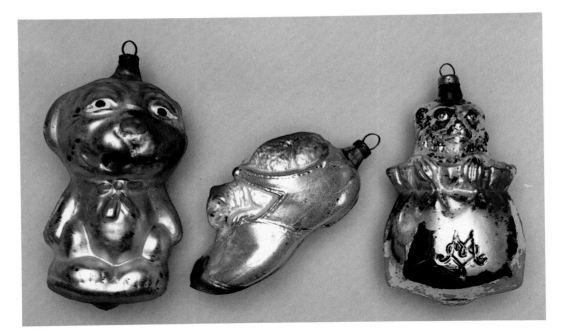

Plate 201. Left: Dog with a ribbon, 1920's, 4". Center: Cat in a shoe, early 1900's, 4". Right: Cat in a bag, 1920's, 4¼".

Plate 202. Left: Two-faced dog (both sides of the ornament are the same), 1½". Right: Cat on a clip, 2¼".

Plate 203. Outline of a cat's face on a popcorn ball head.

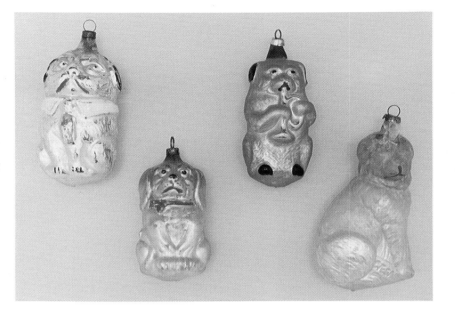

Plate 204. Left: Dog with ear muffs, 3½". Left center: Seated Spaniel with red ribbon, 3". Right center: Dog with a trumpet, 3½". Right: Dog sitting with head turned (has been named Caesar), 4".

Plate 205. Left: Scotty, 1920's, 4". Center: Begging dog, early 1900's to 1930's, 3¾". Right: Dog in "My Darling" bag, 1920's to 1930's, 3".

Plate 206. Left: Bear with a muff, 3¾". Left center: Large bear with a stick, 3¾". Right center: Bear in a clown suit, 4". Right: Small bear with a stick, 2½".

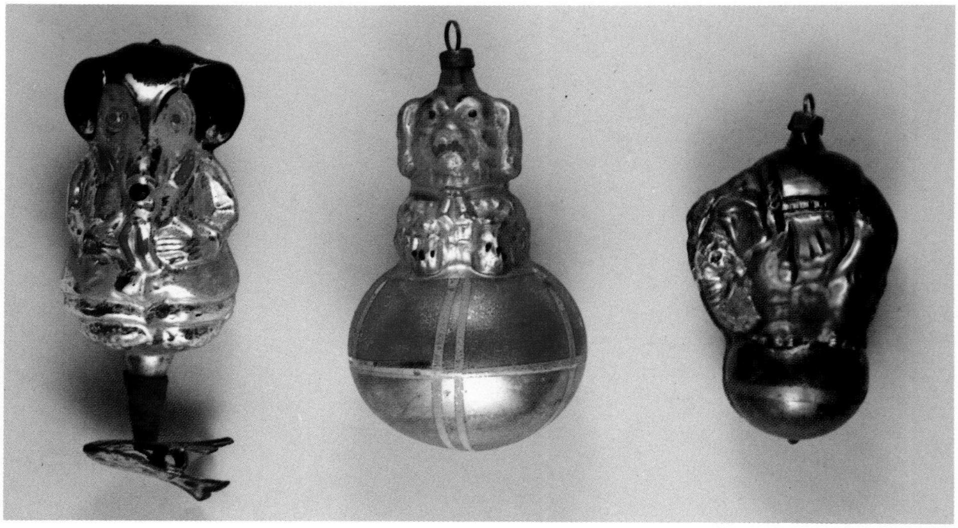

Plate 207. Mouse on a clip, 1920's, 4".
Center: Dog on a ball, 1930's, 3½".
Right: Elephant on a ball, 1920's to
1930's, 2¾".

Plate 208. Left: Pig with flower on stomach,
4". Center: Monkey with a ruffled collar,
3". Right: Bear with a club, 2½".

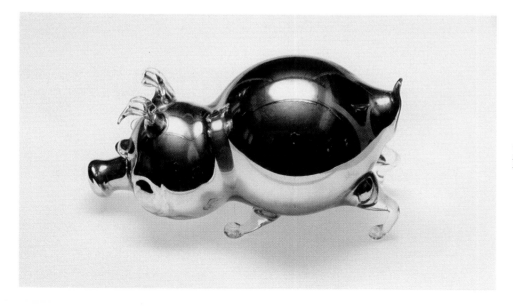

Plate 209. Silver pig ornament, 5½"
long.

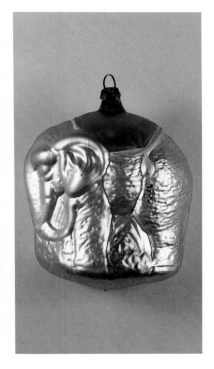

Plate 210. Standing elephant, late 1800's to 1920's, 3¼".

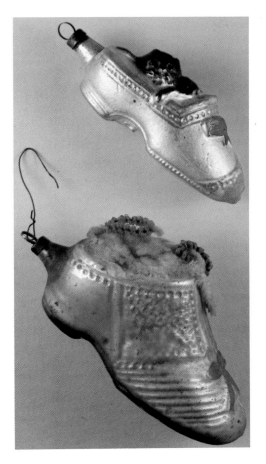

Plate 211. Top: Cat in shoe, early 1900's, 3¼" long. Bottom: Glass shoe with cotton lining, early 1900's, 4¾" long.

Plate 212. Radio monkey, 1920's to 1930's, 4½".

Plate 213. Left: Embossed rabbit, 2¾". Center: Hedgehog, 4" long. Right: Chick on a nest, 3".

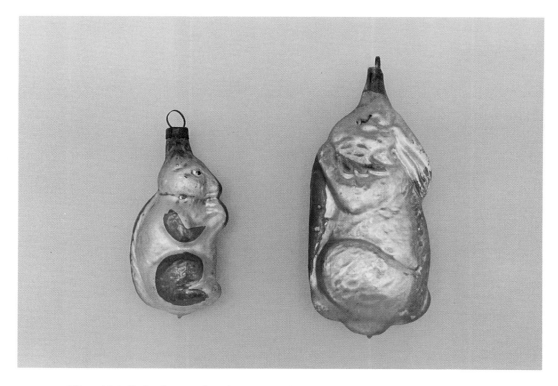

Plate 214. Left: Squirrel with a nut, 2½". Right: Rabbit eating a carrot, 4".

Plate 215. Left: Blown white milk glass fox on a clip, 3". Right: Blown white milk glass deer on a clip, 2½".

Plate 216. Left: Small blown silver color deer, 3½". Center: Large blown silver color deer with long glass antlers, 6". Right: Large gold color blown deer, 5½".

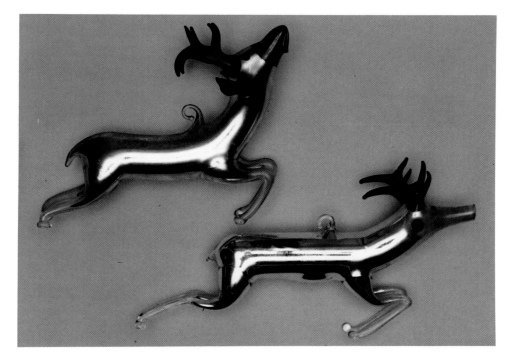

Plate 217. Blown silver color deer with short black antlers, circa 1930's, 4½" to 5".

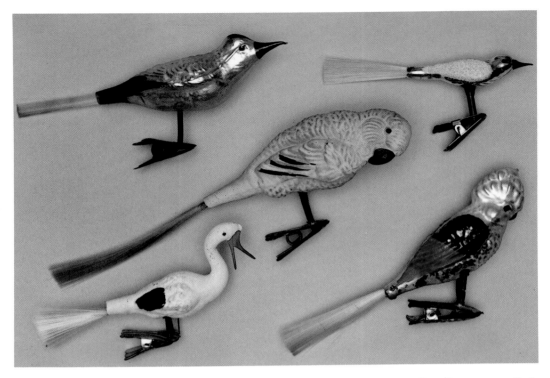

Plate 218. Among the figural ornaments, birds are the most common. Parakeets are a little more difficult to find than common songbirds. Many bird ornaments will have spun glass wings and spring clip fasteners.

Plate 219. The hummingbird with the spun glass wings is a little unusual. The turkey on the bottom right is rather elongated and odd-looking.

78

Plate 220. Left: Molded peacock on a clip, 4". Center: Chick on a clip, 2½". Right: Mother, father and three baby birds in a nest, 3½".

Plate 221. Peacock ornaments gave decorators a chance to express their artistic skills. Many brightly decorated peacocks were made in the 1920's and 1930's.

Plate 222. Owls were a symbol of wisdom, and these ornaments were made in many shapes and sizes during the early twentieth century. Older owls have more detailed molding than newer ones.

Plate. Left: Bird perched at bird-house, 1920's, 2¾". Center: Bird sitting on branch, 1920's, 2¼". Right: Bird with wings spread perched on branch, 1920's, 2¼".

Plate 224. Left: Red bird on branch, early 1900's, 2". Right: Songbird at birdhouse, early 1900's, 3".

Plate 225. Left: Standing duck, 3". Center: Seated turkey, 3". Right: Embossed turkey, 2½".

80

Plate 226. Left: Embossed parrot, 3".
Right: Eagle head, 3½".

Plate 227. Left: Birdcage with embossed red bird, 3¼". Left center: Birdcage with embossed red bird on red branch, 3¼". Right center: Birdcage with embossed blue bird, 3¼". Right: Birdcage with embossed bird, 2¼".

Plate 228. Left: Hexagonal carousel with embossed animal figures, 3¼". Right: Four-sided carousel with embossed animal figures, 2½".

Plate 229. Left: Twin clip-on storks with open beaks and spun glass tails, 4" long. Left center: Large stork with closed beak and spun glass tail, 5½" long. Right center: Twin clip-on canaries with spun glass tails, 7" long. Right: Large clip-on stork with open beak and spun glass tail, 6" long.

Plate 230. Left: Blown crane with blue body, 4½". Right: Blown crane with silver body, 5¾".

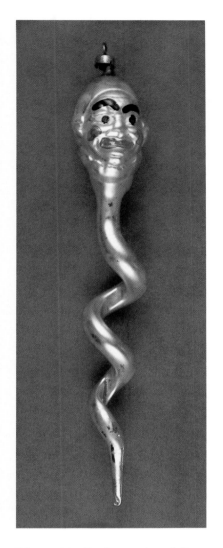

Plate 231. Snake, painted face and curled body, late 1800's to 1930's, 7" long.

Plate 232. Small goldfish are commonly found tree ornaments. They were produced in abundance from the late 1800's until 1930's. Many of the newer ornaments lack the mold and paint detail of the earlier ornaments. These fish are 4" and 4½" long.

Plate 233. Wire-wrapped fish are not as common as other fish.

Plate 234. Left: Shark with spun glass tail, 7" long. Right: Seahorse, 4½".

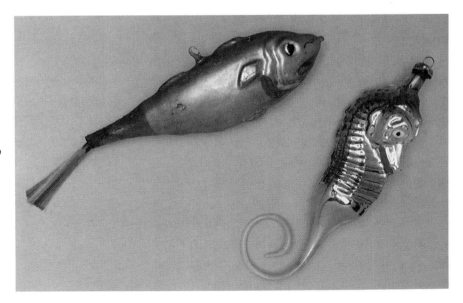

83

Plate 235. The gold fish on the right with the pink face is a puffer. It is about 2½" in diameter. The pink and blue fish in the center are angel fish. The large one measures 4", and the small one 2¼". The fish with the red waves on its side is unusual. It is 5" long.

Plate 236. Left: Anchor with a scrap decoration, 5½". Center: Steamship with a Dresden paper anchor. Right: Mermaid, 4¼".

Plate 237. Left: Common frog, 4". Right: Singing frog with open mouth, 3¾".

Plate 238. Open seashell with pearl, 1920's, 3" high.

Plate 239. Silver frog on a ball, 5½" long.

Plate 240. Beetle on a fruit, 3" high.

Plate 241. Top: Embossed butter-fly, 2½". Center: Embossed beetle, 2¼". Bottom: Embossed butterfly on an indented ornament, 2½".

Plate 242. Left: Embossed but-terfly, early 1900's, 2¼". Center: Lady bug, early 1900's, 2¾". Right: Embossed moth, early 1900's, 2¼".

86

Plate 244. Butterfly with a solid glass body and spun glass wings; 2½" long; wingspan, 4".

Plate 243. Moths with blown glass bodies and spun glass wings; large moth has leather hinges on wings. Small 2¼" long; large, 3½" long.

Plate 245. Left: Butterfly with green spun glass wings; 3½" long; wingspan, 3". Right: Butterfly with yellow wings; 3" long; 4" wingspan.

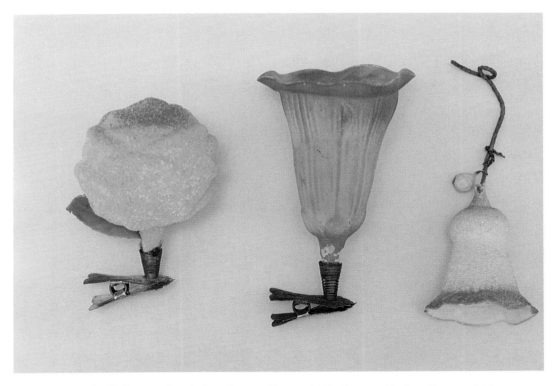

Plate 246. Left: Yellow and red closed rose clip-on, 3½". Center: Red, yellow and blue trumpet flower clip-on, 4". Right: Small red, white and blue trumpet flower on a string, 2½".

Plate 247. Left: Candle clip ornament with glass shade, early 1900's, 3". Center: Flower bud, unsilvered, early 1900's, 3". Right: Unsilvered open rose with stamen exposed, early 1900's, 3¾".

Plate 248. Early unsilvered flowers and candle clip ornaments are not easily found. Candle clips are about 3½".

Plate 249. Left: Rose candle clip, 3¼". Center: Silver rose with exposed pistils, 3½". Right: Floral candle clip ornament with extended pistils, 3¾".

Plate 250. Left: Closed trumpet flower candle clip, 3¼". Right: Open glass ornament with cloth flowers, 2½".

Plate 251. Red rose, unsilvered, diameter 2½".

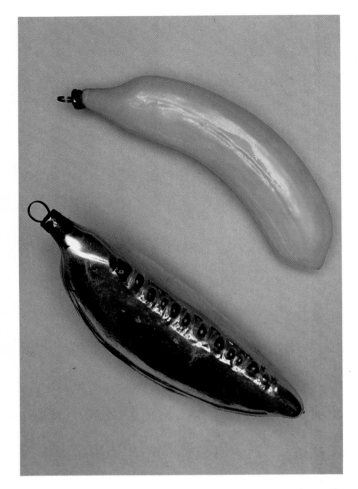

Plate 252. Top: Banana, unsilvered, early 1900's, 4½". Bottom: Watermelon slice, silvered, early 1900's to 1930, 5½".

Plate 253. Top left: Embossed acorns, height, 2¼". Top right: Embossed rose, 3¼". Bottom left: Embossed cherries, 3¼". Bottom right: Embossed grapes, 3½".

Plate Left: Three-sided ornament with embossed cherries, 3½". Center: Large ornament with three embossed cherries, 4". Right: Leaves with cherries, 3¾".

Plate 255. a. Fruit cluster, red, 3"; b. Pineapple, 3½"; c. Strawberry, silver with red leaves, 2"; d. Radish, 3¾"; e. Peach, 3½"; f. Strawberry, pink, 2½"; g. Banana, unsilvered, 4".

Plate 256. a. Orange, unsilvered, 2"; b. Lemon, unsilvered, 2¼"; c. Orange, unsilvered, 2".

Plate 257. Left: Orange, circa 1920's, 2". Center: Peach, 1920's to 1930's, 3¾". Right: Lemon, 1920's, 4".

Plate 258. Left: Pear, early 1900's to 1930's, 4". Center: Tomato, early 1900's to 1920's, 2¾". Right: Strawberry, 1920's, 3¼".

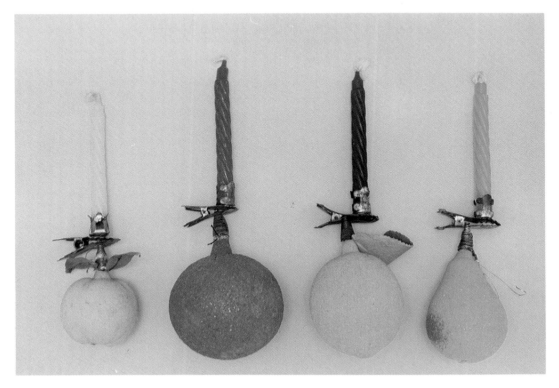

Plate 259. Fruit candle clips decorated with mica. a. Peach, 3¾"; b. Orange, 4½"; c. Lemon, 4½"; d. Pear, 4".

Plate 260. Left: Orange with crinkled skin, 2½". Center: Tomato, 2¼". Right: Orange with textured skin, 3½".

Plate 261. Left: Apple clip-on candleholder coated with mica, 4". Center: Pear clip-on candleholder, 6¼"; Right: Peach clip-on candleholder coated with mica, 4".

Plate 262. Top left: Cone, loaded with goodies, 6". Top right: Cornucopia filled with toys, 4". Bottom left: Flower basket, 2¾". Bottom right: Fruit basket, 3¾".

93

Plate 263. Left: Wirewrapped cluster of grapes, early 1900's to 1930's, 4¼". Right: Wirewrapped pinecone, early 1900's, 3½".

Plate 264. Red grape clusters. The newer one on the left is from West Germany. The one on the right is from the 1930's, 3½".

Plate 265. From left: a. Berry cluster, 3"; b. Berry cluster, 3¾"; c. Peas in a pod, 3"; d. Strawberry, 2".

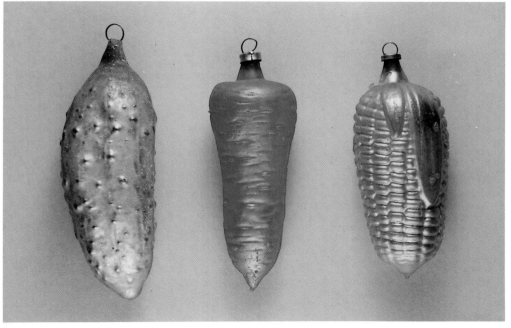

Plate 266. Left: Pickle, silvered, 1900 to 1930's, 4". Center: Carrot, 1920's to 1930's, 3½". Right: Ear of corn, silvered, 1900 to 1930's, 3½".

Plate 267. Left: Potato, 3¼". Center: Ear of corn, silvered, 5". Right: Clip-on squash, 3½".

Plate 268. Miniature ear of Indian corn – red with green leaves, 2".

Plate 269. Left: Large triple mushroom, 4¼". Center: Single mushroom, 3½". Right: Large mushroom with cluster of small mushrooms, 2½".

Plate 270. Clip-on mushroom, unsilvered, 1920's, 3¼".

Plate 271. Replicas of acorns, walnuts, and various other tree fruits have been made as ornaments. The small red acorn measures 1½", and the large silver walnut is 2½" high.

Plate 272. Pinecones were popular ornaments for early trees and are still used by many people today. As a result of this popularity, they enjoyed a long period of production from the late 1800's until the present. Expect early ornaments to have sharply molded features. The cones in this picture range in size from 1½" to 4".

Plate 273. Various examples of ornaments with multiple arms may be found. They usually have moveable acorns, cones, or bells hanging from these arms. Most were made from the early 1920's to the mid 1930's.

Plate 274. Pine trees on clips are common holiday decorations. The tree in the center is decorated with ornaments. 4½" high; 1920's to 1930's.

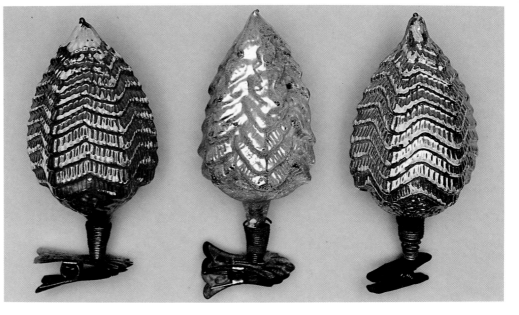

Plate 275. Left: Decorated Christmas tree, 4". Right: Decorated Christmas tree, red, 3½".

Plate 276. Left: Horn, length, 4½". Right: Pipe, 4¾" long.

Plate 277. Top left: Lyre with scrap angel, 1920's to 1930's, 4½". Top right: Horn, painted and silvered, 6½". Bottom left: Guitar 1920's to 1930's, 4". Bottom right: Horn, 3¾".

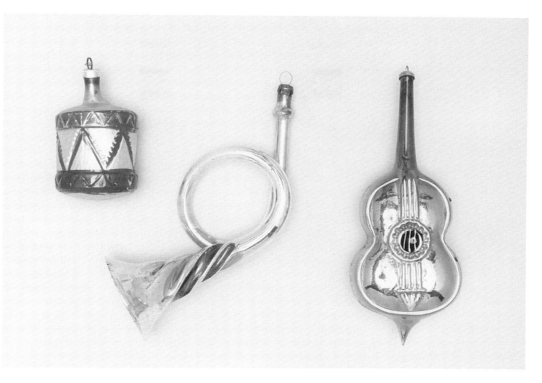

Plate 278. a. Drum, 2½"; b. Horn, 6"; c. Cello, 5¾".

Plate 279. Silvered ornaments with arms utilizing scrap for decoration. Left: Arm with scrap Santa decoration, 4½". Center: Arm with scrap hand with floral bouquet, 5". Right: Arm with Dresden butterfly, 3½".

Plate 280. a. Ocean liner, 2¾"; b. Automobile, 3½"; c. Square-shape car, 2¼".

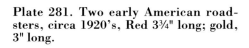

Plate 281. Two early American roadsters, circa 1920's, Red 3¾" long; gold, 3" long.

Plate 282. Top: Early sedan, circa 1920's, 3¼" long. Bottom: Early coupe, circa 1920's, 4" long.

100

Plate 283. a. Red coupe, 3¼";
b. Silver and red "Funny
Car," 3¼"; c. Blue sedan, 3¼".

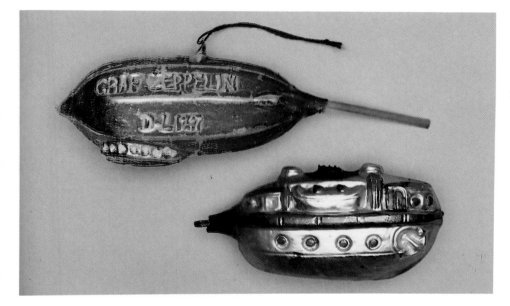

Plate 284. Top: Graf Zeppelin, DL-127; 1920's, 5" long. Bottom: Steamship, early 1900's, 4" long.

Plate 285. Zeppelin "Los Angeles," 1920's, 5" long.

101

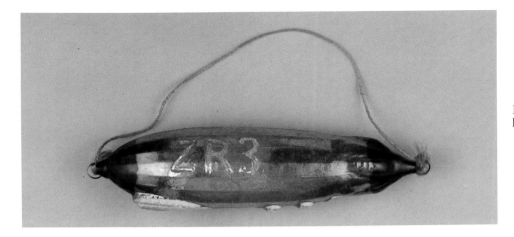

Plate 286. Zeppelin ZR-3, 1920's, 5½" long.

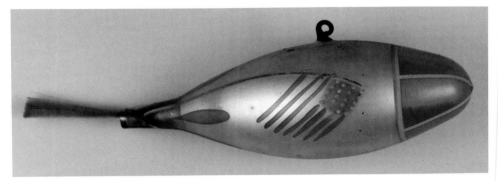

Plate 287. Zeppelin with US flag and spun glass tail, circa late 1920's, 5" long.

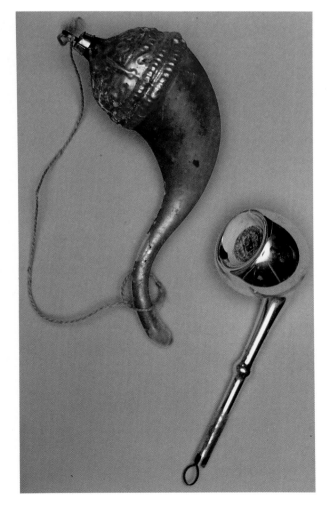

Plate 288. Top: Bent Dublin-style pipe, early 1900's, 5" long. Bottom: Pipe, possibly 1930's, 4" long.

Plate 289. Silver shoe with red and green trim, 4¾".

Plate 290. Left: Church, circa 1920's, 4¼" high. Center: Cottage with a pine tree, early 1900's to 1930's, 3¾" high. Right: Cottage with turkey in front, 1920 to 1930's, 3¾" high.

Plate 291. Top row: a. Silver house with red roof, 2¼": b. House embossed on an oval, 3"; c. House with tree embossed at side of roof, 3". Bottom row: a. Town hall with steeple, 3¼"; b. House with green tree at front door, 3"; c. Bell with embossed windmill, 2¼".

Plate 292. Left: Tower with silver top, 4¼". Right: Tower with snow top, 4".

Plate 293. Left: Windmill, 1920's, 3" high. Center: Guardhouse or outhouse, 1920's to 1930's, 3" high. Right: Lighthouse, 1920's and 1930's, 3½" high.

Plate 294. Left: Outhouse under a star, 5½" high. Right: Lighthouse, 4" high.

Plate 295. Candle on a clip, 5" high.

Plate 296. Left: Pocket watch, 2". Right: Cuckoo clock with paper face, early 1900 to 1920's, 3½" high.

Plate 297. Top row: a. Bell with round embossed top. 3¾"; b. Bell with square embossed top, 3½"; c. Bell embossed "Merry Christmas," 3". Bottom row: a. Beaded swirl, red and gold bell, 2"; b. Red, white and blue bell, 2"; c. Ornament with embossed bells, 2½".

Plate 298. Teapots and sugars were common household items which were copied by ornament designers. Many exotic shapes have been found.

Plate 299. Left: Gold teapot with embossed flower, 2½". Center: Pink teapot with green leaf, 2½". Right: Silver teapot with embossed flower, 2".

Plate 300. Teapot and coffee pot sold as part of a series of ornaments with a similar finish by Montogomery Ward during the 1950's.

Plate 301. Left: Ornament with an embossed rope, 3¾". Center: Ornament with embossed cherubs, 4¼". Right: Barrel with embossed flowers, 3¼".

Plate 302. Lamp ornaments were made in many sizes and shapes during the 1920's and 1930's.

Plate 303. Various colors of miniature basket-type ornaments, 1" high.

Plate 304. Left: Money bag with embossed flowers, 2½". Right: Money bag embossed "50000.," 2¾".

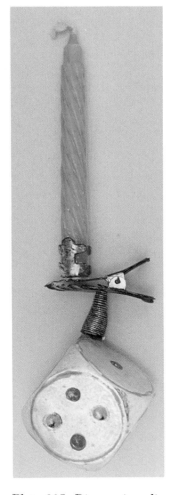

Plate 307. Football, early 1900's.

Plate 305. Dice spring-clip candleholder, 2½".

Plate 306. Telephone, circa 1940's, 2".

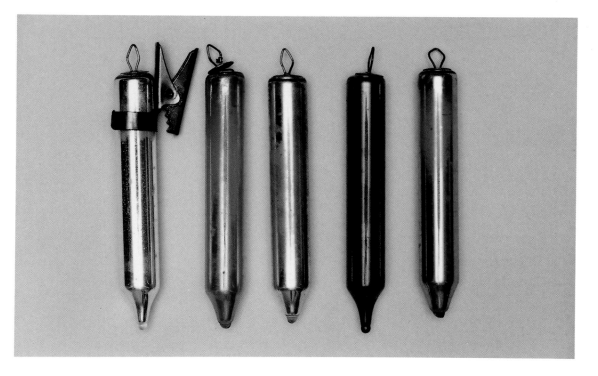

Plate 308. Glass candles, with clips, 1940's, 3½".

Plate 309. Glass icicles, circa, 1950's, 14" long.

Plate 310. Glass icicles, 5" long.

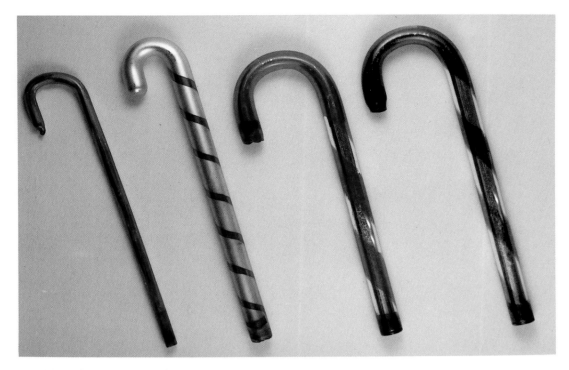

Plate 311. Glass candy canes. Left: diameter 1¼", 7" long; Right: diameter ⅜", 6¼" long.

Plate 312. Occupied Japan glass bead ornaments.

Plate 313. Czechoslavakian glass bead ornaments.

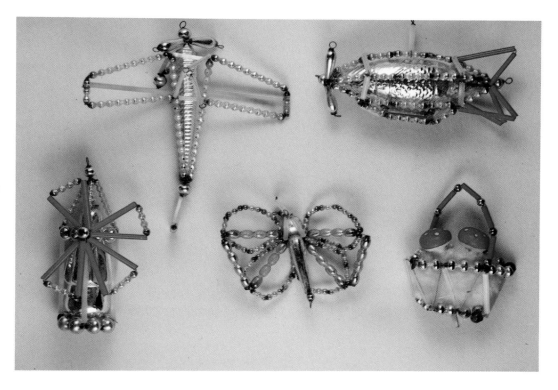

Plate 314. Czechoslavakian glass bead ornaments.

Plate 315. Large wreath-shaped Czech ornament with glass candle, 7½" high.

Plate 316. Boxed set of satin bells, circa 1950's.

Plate 317. Boxed set of garland type beads made in Japan, circa 1950's.

Plate 318. Early garland string, 28" long.

Plate 319. Ornate glass garland string, 60" long.

112

Plate 320. Glass ornamental garland, 36" long.

Plate 321. Short garland, 24" long.

Plate 322. Short strings of glass balls used to hang from branches, 8" to 12" long.

113

Plate 323. Hanging glass ornament, 12" long.

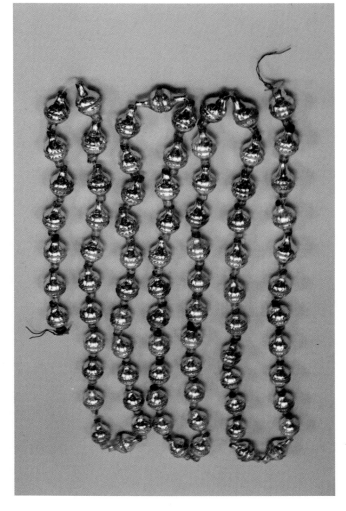

Plate 324. Very long glass tree garland dating from the 1950's, 110" long.

Plate 325. 1950's glass bead tree garland, 110" long.

114

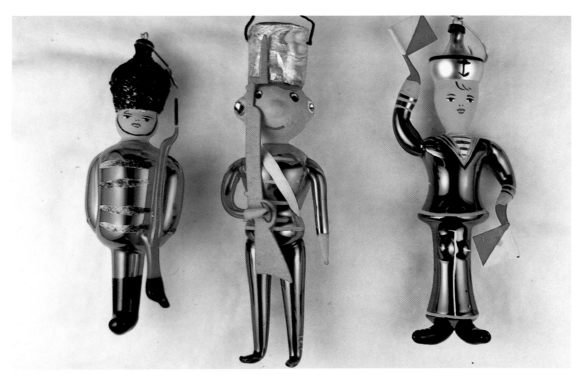

Plate 326. Italian military figurals, circa 1950's to 1970's, 6" high.

Plate 327. Late Italian figurals including Peter Pan, 6" high.

115

Plate 328. Italian clown, harlequin, and Indian were made during the last thirty years, 6" high.

Plate 329. Modern Italian representation of a spaceman and spaceship.

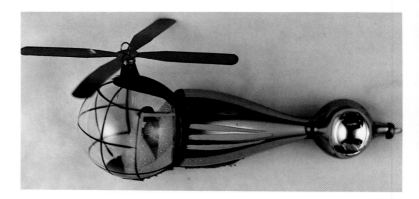

Plate 330. Italian helicopter, 8" long.

Plate 331. Mouse, probably late European.

116

Wire – Wrapped Glass Ornaments

Glass ornaments which are encased in a thin crinkly wire are called "wire-wrapped" ornaments. Ornaments of this type were first produced in the last half of the 1800's and were very popular during the Victorian era. These early ornaments were usually unsilvered and elaborately wrapped. These ornaments are very delicate, and, therefore, few have survived.

Wire-wrapped ornaments produced later – after 1900 – were usually silvered. With these ornaments, as with their predecessors, Dresden paper, "chromos," or other materials were usually used to produce a finished ornament.

Wire-wrapped ornaments were crafted in an array of subjects. Favorite subjects for wrapping were ornaments depicting forms of transportation such as ships or balloons. Other wire-wrapped ornaments commonly found include musical instruments, birdcages, and parasols.

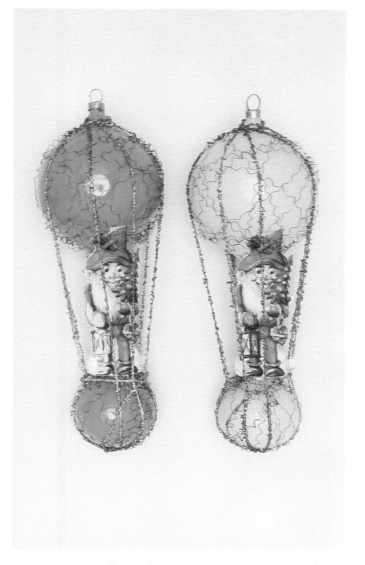

Plate 332. Left: Scrap figure on a wire-wrapped red balloon, 6½". Right: Scrap figure on a wire-wrapped yellow balloon, 6½".

Plate 333. Left: "Chromo" figure on a wire-wrapped ball. Right: Wire-wrapped boat with sail.

Plate 334. Left: Angelic "chromo" figure on a wire-wrapped ball. Right: "Chromo" figure on a wire-wrapped ball.

Plate 335. Santa scrap heads on Victorian wire-wrapped airplanes; Blue and gold, 6¼"; Red, 7".

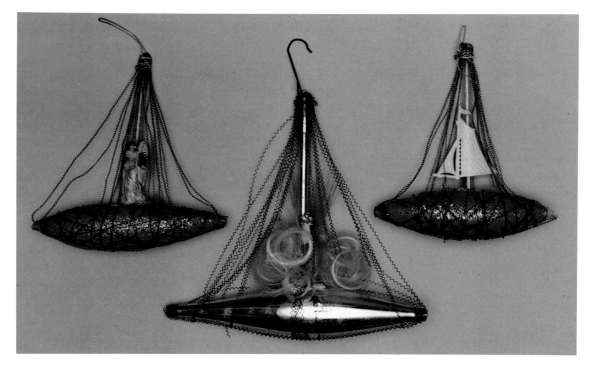

Plate 336. Left: "Chromo" angel riding blue wire-wrapped boat, 5" high. Center: Silver wire-wrapped boat with mushroom and spun glass, 6" high. Right: Blue wire-wrapped boat with paper sail, 5" high.

Plate 337. Left: Wire-wrapped Victorian steamship, 5". Center: Victorian fruit vase, 6½". Right: Scrap santa head on a Victorian dirigible, 4".

Plate 338. Wire-wrapped spider in a web.

Plate 339. Left: Wire-wrapped basket with a feather tree, 4". Right: Wire-wrapped umbrella with a paper flower, 4".

Plate 340. Fancy early German wire-wrapped umbrella.

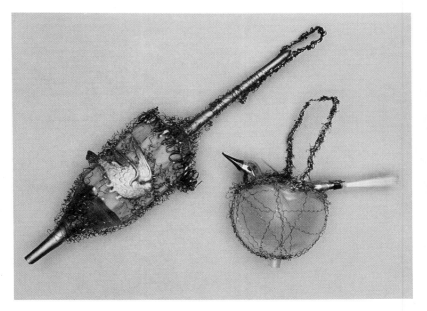

Plate 341. Left: Wire-wrapped birdcage with paper Dresden bird, 9" high. Right: Wire-wrapped nest with glass bird, 4" long.

Plate 342. Left: Wire-wrapped bell with Dresden paper leaf, 4" high. Right: Wire-wrapped bell, 5½" high.

Plate 343. Wire-wrapped swans, 4" long.

Plate 344. Left: Wire-wrapped chandelier, 5" high. Right: Early wire-wrapped ornament, 6" high.

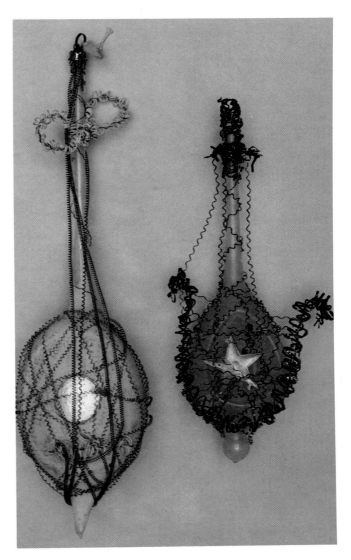

Plate 345. Two wire-wrapped mandolins. Left, 5" long; Right, 4" long.

Plate 346. Left: Wire-wrapped flower pot, 5" high. Center: Wire-wrapped vase, 6" high. Right: Wire-wrapped flower pot, 5" high.

Plate 347. Left: Wire-wrapped horn. Center: Wire-wrapped violin. Right: Fancy wire-wrapped bottle.

Plate 348. Left: Wire-wrapped open umbrella, 5½" high. Center: Wire-wrapped closed umbrellas, 9½" high. Right: Wire-wrapped Santa scrap on ball, 5½" high.

Plate 349. Left: Glass bead and tinsel combination. Right: Father Christmas and tinsel combination.

Plate 350. Left: Tinsel and glass ball combination with the addition of a "chromo" Father Christmas head. Right: Glass container completely enveloped with tinsel to form a basket.

Glass and Tinsel Combinations

Many interesting ornaments were made of glass and tinsel in the United States in the late 1800's and the early 1900's. The basic shape of the ornament was formed from tinsel rope. Small glass balls were suspended from these structures with the use of thin wires. Production of the ornaments continued until their popularity declined in the late 1920's.

Plate 351. Top: Large glass and tinsel ornament, 9" high. Bottom: Diamond-shape glass and tinsel ornament, 7" high.

Plate 352. These special bulbs were produced to hold "chromos." Father Christmas figures are encased in these two bulbs. 5½" high.

Plate 353. This bulb was specially designed to be completed by this "chromo" torso and legs. The combination makes a very attractive ornament.

Plate 354. Spun glass and Dresden sunburst with a wax baby, 5".

Plate 355. Spun glass ornament with a scrap face, 5½".

Scrap and Spun Glass Ornaments

Die-cuts were often produced in such a manner that other elements were necessary to complete the figure. Many times spun glass was selected to fulfill this requirement. The more common ornaments are made with angel scraps and have skirts completed with spun glass. Others feature Father Christmas torsos and boots with spun glass robes. Some spun glass and scrap ornaments were designed to be used as tree top decorations. The most commonly found color of spun glass is white. However, diligent searching will uncover spun glass ornaments with yellow, blue, or green glass.

Plate 356. Father Christmas scrap combined with spun glass, 9½" high.

Plate 357. Father Christmas scrap and spun glass combination form a tree ornament, 9½" high.

Plate 358. Angel scraps used in combination with spun glass. The ornament on the left is for the tree top, and is probably from the late 1940's since it was made in Western Germany. Left: 6"; Center: 4½"; Right: 3".

Plate 359. The two angels in this ornament have their flared skirts completed with spun glass, 6" high.

Plate 360. Left: Spun glass and scrap combination ornament. Santa has a long spun glass beard. Right: Spun glass tree top ornament featuring Father Christmas, diameter 8".

Plate 361. Left: Ornament with girl in a wreath of roses, girl's skirt is made from spun glass, 5½". Right: Tree top ornament made from spun glass with a large angel in the center, diameter 8".

Scrap and Tinsel Ornaments

Paper figures, popularly called "scraps," were often combined with tinsel to produce tree ornaments. The number of combinations for this type of ornament is almost endless. Thousands of designs were made commercially, and vast numbers of ornaments were made at home. Because of their durability, scrap and tinsel ornaments were promoted with much aggressiveness by the early mail order companies. The popularity of these ornaments was greatest in the early 1900's and began to decline by World War I.

Plate 362. A trace of the original cellophane is still attached to this scrap and tinsel ornament which features Father Christmas, 9" high.

Plate 363. The sinister look on this scrap Father Christmas would scare many young children, 9" high.

Plate 364. This scrap and tinsel ornament features Father Christmas in a heart-shaped scrap, 6" high.

Plate 365. Children were the subject of many scraps. This scrap only uses a trace of tinsel to form an ornament, 6" high.

Plate 366. Children are the central figures in this scrap and tinsel ornament, 6" high.

Plate 367. These two ornaments combine angel scraps with tinsel to form decorations. Left, 6½"; Right, 4".

Plate 368. Originally, cellophane formed the background of these scrap and tinsel ornaments, 4½" to 6½" high.

Plate 369. This ornament incorporates a cute scrap with children, tinsel, and a small glass ball to form the decoration, 8" high.

Plate 370. Top: St. Nicholas is resting on a key design formed by tinsel, 7½" high. The ornament on the right uses a combination of cotton, cardboard, tinsel, and scraps to form a decoration, 7½" high.

Plate 371. Many candy containers were designed to be hung on the tree. The container on the bottom is made of thin cloth and decorated with scraps and tinsel. The container on the top is made of cloth net and also has tinsel and scrap decorations.

Plate 372. The glass and tinsel ornament on the left has a wire-wrapped glass ball in the center, 7½" long. The candy container cornucopia is a tree ornament which is decorated with scraps and tinsel, 9" long.

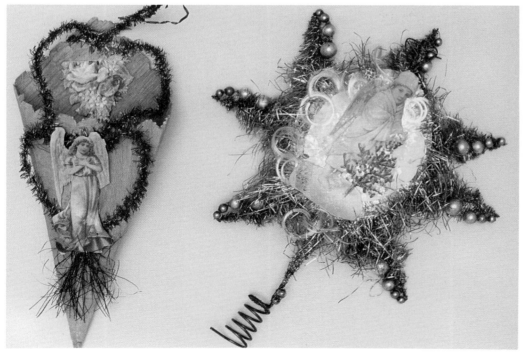

Plate 373. Left: Scrap and tinsel decorated paper cornucopia, 8½" high. Right: Scrap and tinsel tree top ornament, diameter 9".

Plate 374. Left: Scrap, tinsel and cotton girl with a flag, 6". Right: Cupid on horseshoe, 7".

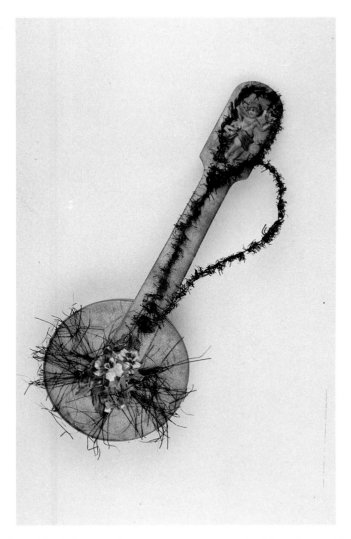

Plate 375. The mandolin ornament formed with this combination of scraps, tinsel, and cardboard is 9" long.

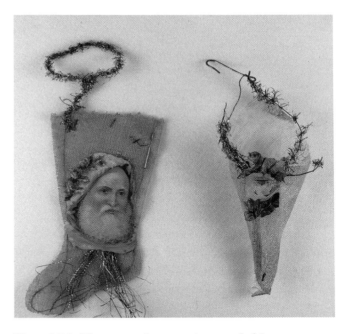

Plate 376. Many candy containers of this type were home made. These two candy containers, which were also used as tree ornaments use a combination of heavy cloth net with scraps and tinsel.

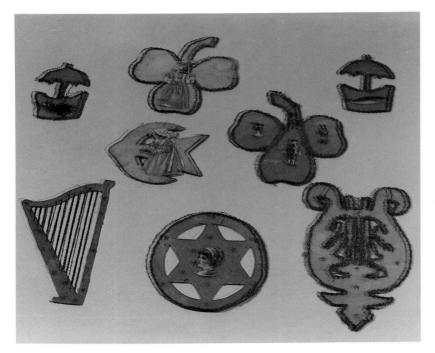

Plate 377. Cotton cut-out forms were often decorated with scraps and tinsel to make ornaments. The largest ornament is 16" high, and the smallest is just over 4".

Cotton Ornaments

During the early 1900's many different cotton batting figures were made for use as Christmas tree ornaments. The earliest versions of these figures were of good quality and were made in Germany. Later figures from the 1920's and 1930's were made in Japan.

Human and animal figures will be found and are often referred to as "cotton wool" ornaments. Some of the figures had cotton bodies with bisque, china, or colored scrap heads. Many of the Japanese figures had plaster faces. The faces, arms, and legs of these figures were often completed with scraps.

Plate 378. Cotton and scraps combined nicely to form elaborate ornaments, 17½" high.

Plate 379. Popular Father Christmas ornaments were made from cotton, scraps and tinsel, 9" high.

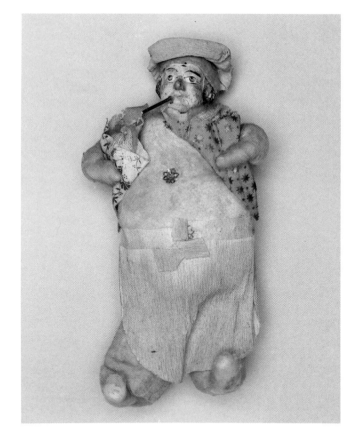

Plate 380. This peasant figure is made of cotton and has a composition face. He is about 5" high.

Plate 381. Many early German cotton ornaments depicted peasant girls. This girl has a crepe paper dress and a scrap face.

Plate 382. White cotton Japanese snow figures on skis, 4¾" high.

Plate 384. These cotton Santa figural ornaments are Japanese. Their faces are plaster. They are 7" high.

Plate 383. A variety of cotton Santa figures were made in Japan. These have plaster faces. The one on the left is 5" high, and the one on the right is 6" high.

Plate 385. Small cotton Santa figures were used to complement simple decorations such as balls. The ball is papiermache.

Plate 386. This is a wrapped cotton Santa with a wire body and composition face, 10½" high.

Plate 387. Cotton figures in swings were convenient forms to hang on trees. The girl has a compostion face and crepe paper skirt. Bear, 2½" high; girl, 3½" high.

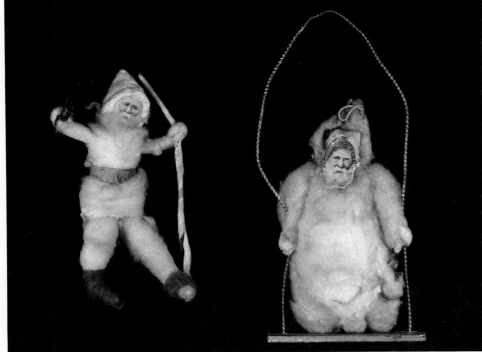

Plate 388. Cotton was combined with many different materials to produce ornaments. The Santa on the left has a composition face, and the one on the right has a scrap face, 3½" high.

Plate 389. These two miniature Santas are enjoying their ride in the clouds. The cotton Santas are just under two inches tall. The ornament on the left is 4" high, and the one on the right is 3½" high.

Plate 390. This early German peasant girl has a cornhusk dress. Her face is composition, and she is 5½" high. The Santa is cotton with a plaster face. He is 4" high.

Plate 391. This cotton batting Santa has a scrap face. He is carrying a feather tree, and he is 6" high.

Plate 392. The snowman on the left is made of cotton batting which is wrapped around a cardboard cylinder. He is about 6" high. The small girl is made of cotton and has a scrap face.

Plate 393. Yarn was a common household item for many families. As a result, some scraps were combined with yarn to form ornaments, 5" high.

Plate 394. German cotton ornaments with a composition face are not easy to find, 4¾" high.

Plate 395. This angel doll ornament has a cotton body and a celluloid face, 4" high.

Plate 396. Early German cotton animals are very collectible. These were made before World War I.

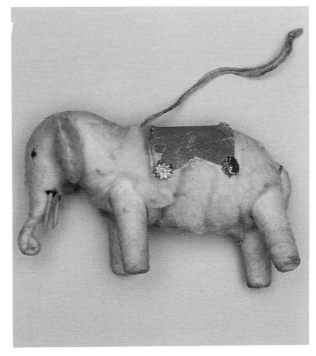

Plate 397. Elephants were among the many types of animal ornaments made of cotton. This elephant is nicely finished with wood tusks and a colorful paper saddle. He is 4½" long.

Pressed Cotton Ornaments

Spun cotton ornaments were promoted for use as unbreakable alternatives for the delicate glass ornaments during the early 1900's. These ornaments were pressed from molds, and the finished pieces were usually dyed to produce a pastel-colored ornament. Fruits and vegetables were especially popular, and these are the ornaments which are found most commonly today. Some of the ornaments were wire-wrapped and leaves were often added to the fruits.

Plate 398. Pressed cotton icicles, 6" long.

Plate 399. Cotton fruit. Top: Small pear, 1½"; Small orange, 1". Center: Orange, 2½"; Pear, 3½". Bottom: Lemon, 3"; Apple, 2".

Plate 400: Top: Wire-wrapped apple, 2";
Carrot, 3"; Turnip, 2½". Bottom: Radish,
2½"; Apple, 2½"; Banana, 6½".

Plate 401. Top: Bell, 1½"; Icicle, 4"; Cham-
pagne bottle, 3". Bottom: Snowman, 3½";
Bell, 1¼"; Bell 1½".

Plate 402. Left to right: Turnips, 4"; Pear,
3½"; Peach, 3"; Beet, 3".

Paper Ornaments

Paper ornaments may be divided into several categories:

1. Dresden paper ornaments were made between 1880 and the early 1900's. They are named for the area of Germany in which they were made. Dresdens are made of silver or gold color embossed cardboard. Most of the finished shapes are these colors. However, some pieces were painted realistic colors. Two different styles of Dresden ornaments will be found: flat and three-dimensional. The flat ornaments are simply lacquered, silver and gold-colored embossed die-cuts. These ornaments will be commonly found in the shape of animals, stars, musical instruments, and birds.

Three dimensional Dresden ornaments are the most collectible and the hardest to find. These gold and silver shapes are made from embossed die-cut cardboard pieces which were glued together and finished by hand. Many of the designs were elaborate, and the finished ornaments often had the same detail as life-like figures. Shapes include human figures, angels, animals, birds, ships, carriages, and many other turn of the century objects.

2. Scraps are chromolithiographed die-cuts which were usually combined with other materials to form a complete ornament. These ornaments were most popular from the 1860's to the 1920's.

3. Small papier-mache figures were made as ornaments. These were often small versions of the popular belsnickles. They were made from the late 1800's to the early 1900's.

4. Pressed cardboard and thin paper ornaments were made in Germany and Japan. Many of the early paper ornaments are covered with Dresden paper. Honeycomb balls and bells made of thin tissue paper first made their appearance in the early 1900's. Many of these folded flat for easy storage. They were made by the American Paper Novelty Company.

Plate 403. Papier-mache belsnickle figure ornaments. Left, 3½" high; Right, 4" high.

Plate 404. German papier-mache Father Christmas head candle holders, 6" high.

142

Plate 405. Medals made of Dresden-type metallic paper, 3" to 3½" high.

Plate 406. Dresden silver coach, 4" high, 6¼" long.

Plate 407. Dresden owl, 4" high.

Plate 408. Dresden eagle, wingspan, 5½".

Plate 409. Dresden lizard, 4¼" long.

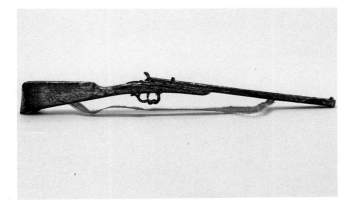

Plate 410. Dresden rifle, 6¼" long.

Plate 411. Dresden paper candy containers, 4" long.

Plate 412. Coated cardboard ornaments. Left: Drum, 2"; Rocking horse, 2½". Right: Baby buggy, 2¼"; Wagon, 2¾".

Plate 413. Red crepe paper Father Christmas ornament on a swing. He has a scrap face and is 5" high.

Plate 414. This is a package tag distributed by the Flower Products Co. of Chicago. The tag was made in Japan and is 3½" in diameter.

Plate 415. These crepe paper bells are marked "A Doubl-Glo product, Made in U.S.A." The large bell is 7" high, and the small bell measures 5".

Plate 416. This ornament is very large. Sometimes these larger ornaments were hung from the ceiling or from mantles. In some cases, ornaments this big were used on large trees. The ornament is comprised of crepe paper, scrap and tinsel, 12" high.

Plate 417. Large crepe paper and scrap ornament, 7" high.

Plate 418. Sometimes scraps were combined with crepe paper to form ornaments. These angels are examples of such ornaments, 6" high.

Plate 419. Small Czechoslavakian cardboard houses designed as tree ornaments are brightly painted and covered with mica, about 1½" high.

Plate 420. Detailed miniature village pieces were often used for decorating trees. These are mica coated, 2¾" high.

Plate 421. These coated cardboard houses make elaborate ornaments with their colorful decorative figures, 1¾" high.

147

Wax and Waxed Ornaments

Along with cookies, apples, candy, and other edibles, wax ornaments are among the earliest of tree decorations. Some of the first wax ornaments were doll-like figures designed as tree top ornaments. These early figures were cast in molds and were made in Germany as early as the beginning of the 1800's. By the mid-nineteenth century other tree decorations were being made from wax. The most common figures are small angels, but other ornaments such as the Christ Child, animals, fruits, and stars were made. Wax is a very fragile substance, and not very many of the old wax ornaments will be found in good condition.

Figures similar to wax ornaments may be found. These decorations have a center of papier-mache or composition and an outer coating of wax. Collectors call wax coated ornaments "waxed" to differentiate between the coated ornaments and their counterparts which are solid wax. The most common waxed ornament found today is an angel about 4" long. Many of these angels have real hair and spun glass wings which are attached by a leather hinge. Other waxed ornaments include flowers, animals, and birds.

Plate 423. Curly blonde hair is more unusual than brown hair. Many angels are equipped with horns, 9" long.

Plate 422. Wax angels usually have real hair. This angel is missing wings and a horn, 11" long.

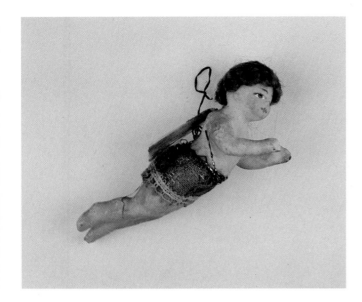

Plate 424. This brown-haired angel is 7" long. The spun glass wings are still intact.

Plate 425. Wax figures can be easily damaged, and many are found in poor condition, 7" long.

Plate 426. Wax and waxed ornaments are usually found in this 4" size. These figures have spun glass wings with leather hinges.

Chenille Ornaments

Candy canes are probably the most commonly found chenille decoration. However, other chenille decorations were made in the shapes of animals, human figures, and bells. Most chenille ornaments are simple and inexpensive, but people are attracted to them because they add a lot of color to their trees.

Plate 427. Left: Santa figure made of chenille with a clay face, 8" high. Right: Chenille candy cane, 5" long.

Plate 428. Chenille candy canes, 12" long.

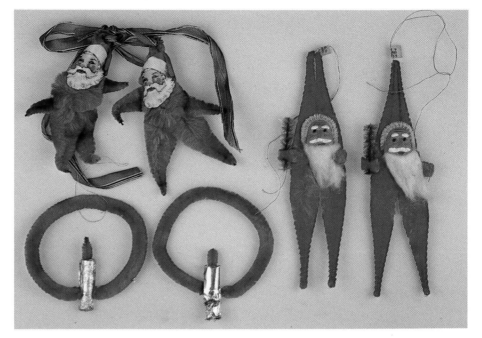

Plate 429. The chenille Santa figures on the left have scrap faces. They are 4" high. The two Santa figures on the right were made in Occupied Japan. They have clay faces and are 6" high. The wreaths are chenille and paper foil. They are 4" in diameter.

Plate 430. Left: Chenille bell with a celluloid Santa face, 4" high. Right: Plain chenille bell, 4½" high.

Plate 431. Chenille, wire, and tinsel were combined to form these cute little ornaments. They are 4" in diameter and were made in the 1950's.

Celluloid and Plastic Ornaments

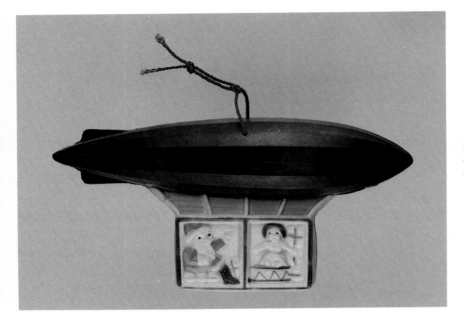

Plate 432. Celluloid ornaments were the forerunners of modern plastic ornaments. The most common celluloid ornaments are birds and other animals. The celluloid dirgible has Santa Claus as a passenger. It is 5" long.

Plate 433. Left: Celluloid bird on a ring, "Japan," 6". Center: Celluloid Santa baby, "Made in Japan," 4". Right: Celluloid Santa in a ring, "Made in U.S.A.," 6".

Plate 434. Assorted plastic ornaments, 3½" to 4" high.

Plate 435. Plastic Pixie ornaments to be used for decorating, 2½" to 3" high.

Plate 436. Plastic ornaments for the tree. These are normally placed above lights. Heat from the lights produces air currents which causes the propellers inside the ornaments to turn.

Metal Ornaments

Metal ornaments were among the earliest of tree decorations. German metal workers began fashioning ornaments from tin and lead as early as the 1700's. Most of the soft tin-lead alloy ornaments which are found today were made before World War I. Other materials such as brass and pewter have also been used to produce metal ornaments. Many of these ornaments will be decorated with glass beads or other colorful materials and most have a shiny lacquer finish to improve their reflective properties. Birdcages, often complete with tiny metal birds, were popular metal decorations.

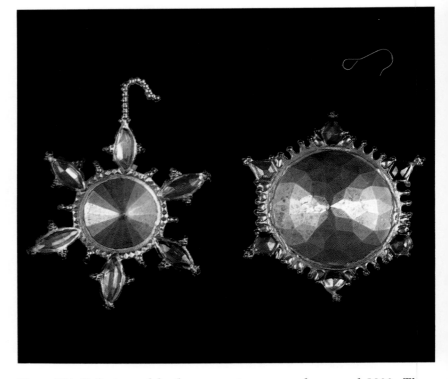

Plate 437. Soft tin and lead ornaments were made around 1900. These ornaments have glass beads and are faceted to improve their reflective qualities, 2½" in diameter.

Plate 438. Shiny plated ornaments reflected the lights from the trees. Left: Birdcage, 2½" high. Right: Basket, 2¼" high.

Plate 439. Metal birdcages often had little metal birds inside. These cages are 3" high.

Plate 440. Small wind-up toys were sometimes used for tree decorations. This little bird and birdcage were made in Germany, 3¼" high.

Plate 441. Various designs of star-shaped decorations may be found. These ornaments from the 1950's are made of tinsel and wire.

Plate 442. Criterion Bell and Specialty company made a tin decoration for miniature trees. The bells looped over the tree and were rung by the movement of the electrical Santa.

Plate 445. The bodies of these figures are made of papier-mache, and the arms are made of wood. The girl has a crepe paper skirt, 4½" high.

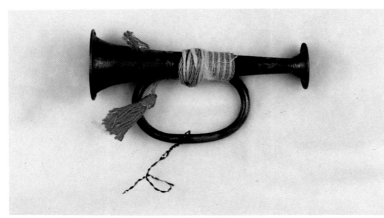

Plate 446. Skilled craftsmen produced hand-made ornaments like this brass horn, 4" long.

Lighting the Christmas Tree
Early Lighting – Candles and Candleholders

The desire to light the Christmas tree probably grew out of man's long-standing relationship with the symbolism of fire and light. Candles were used by early pagans to aid the sun in its return to power during their mid-winter ceremonies. However, burning candles have also been associated with Christ since the first days of the Christian church. They took on the symbolism of Christ as the "Light of the World" in the Christian celebrations.

The earliest records of candles used in the celebration of Christmas establish that candles were used on the pyramid structures in southern Germany. Soon the candles migrated from the pyramid and began appearing on trees.

The first candles were attached to the trees by either tying them to the tree or by allowing a little hot wax to drop on a branch. The candle was then fastened to the drop of wax as it cooled. Later, needle-like pins were inserted into the end of the candle, and the pins were attached to the branches. None of these methods were very secure or safe, and constant attempts were being made to develop a better fastener.

By the mid-nineteenth century metal pins with plates to catch the wax drippings were being used. About this same time tin lanterns with glass windows and heavy glass jars started to appear. The lanterns were designed as a cage which held the candle securely. The glass jars held a layer of water. Oil and a wick were allowed to burn on top of water. These new devices were safer; however, their weight posed a problem for their use as tree ornaments.

By the end of the Civil War new candle-holding devices were being introduced. The first to appear were holders having long wires with weighted balls at the end. These were placed on the trees and were "guaranteed" to hold the candle upright. A short time later spring-clip candleholders were invented. These proved to be very successful and became the most widely used design until the disappearance of candles from trees in the 1920's.

The popularity of spring-clip candleholders led to the introduction of many different designs of this type of holder. The most simple ones are merely a spring with a piece of tin attached. Some more elaborate ones are painted tin in the shapes of animals or flowers. The most sophisticated ones are double-sided with chromolithographed figures such as angels, butterflies, or Santa Claus.

Another type of spring-clip candleholder made an appearance around the turn of the century. These holders had glass shades and were very pretty. However, since the heat of the candles caused many of the shades to crack, they only enjoyed limited success. (For examples of some of these ornaments see the section on glass ornaments.)

The many fires from the lit candles on Christmas trees led to numerous public campaigns against the use of candles. Several factors increased the danger of tree fires in the twentieth century. Trees were drying out more quickly due to better heated houses. Trees were also dryer, because they were now being cut earlier and shipped from greater distances. As a result, these dryer trees caught fire much more easily. America was also becoming electrified, and everyone from insurance companies to the President began endorsing the switch from candles to the much safer electric lights. By the 1920's very few Christmas trees were lit by candles.

Plate 446. Notice the original shade on the jar in the center. These shades are not easy to find. The jars were used for burning oil on water. They are 3½" to 4" high. The cobalt grape jar and the jar with the face are marked "Hearn-wright and Co. Makers." The white milk glass holder and the two holders on the right are outstanding examples of early lamps. Jars like these with embossed figures are very hard to find.

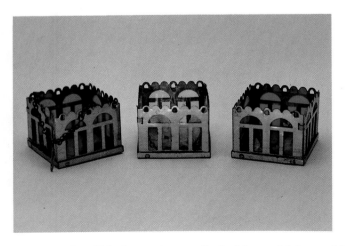

Plate 445. Small lightweight candle-holders which would contain the wax drippings and hold the candle securely were devised for use on trees. These holders from the 1920's are 2" high and are marked "Made in Germany."

Plate 447. These glass jars come in a variety of colors. Some are signed "BROCK'S Crystal Palace Lamp" and were made in Austria. Others are marked "BROCK'S Illumination" and were made in France, 4" high.

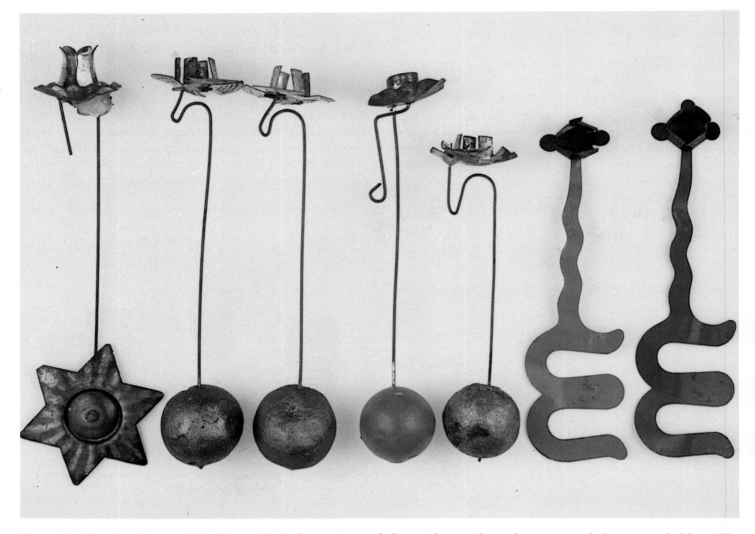

Plate 448. The first five candleholders with the long wires and the weights on the end are counterbalance-type holders. The weights were designed to balance the weight of the candle and hold it straight on the tree. The two holders on the right are extension candleholders. They were attached to the tree and held the candle away from the branches. They range in size from 4" to 6".

Plate 449. The most desirable of the spring-type candles are the double-sided ones with enameled Father Christmas figures. These are 2¼" high.

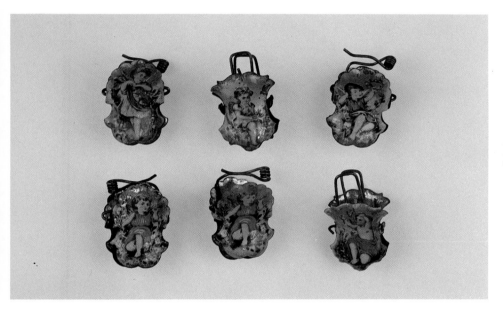

Plate 450. These double-sided angel candle clips are 1½" high.

Plate 451. Angel and cupid figures on candle clips were very popular. These are double-sided clips which are very attractive. Left: Star-shaped angel, 2". Center: Angel, 3". Right: Cupid on elbows, 2½".

Plate 452. Many floral and flower pot varieties of candle clips were produced. These are 1½" high.

Plate 453. Spring-type candle clips were made in many different shapes and sizes. Many were enameled. Top: Angel, 3"; Father Christmas, 2⅜"; Enameled farm scene, 2½". Center: Pinecone, 2¼"; Squirrel, 2"; Butterfly, 1"; Butterfly, 1¾". Bottom: Enameled floral, 1½" Unenameled, 1¾"; Enameled long, 2½"; Bird, 2¼".

Plate 454. Early candle clips were made in different shapes and sizes. Some of the tin clips were enameled, but many were just plain, 1" to 2" long.

160

The Miracle of Electricity

Only a few short years after Edison invented the light bulb, one of his business associates adapted the first electric lamps for use on a Christmas tree. According to a report in the *Detroit Post and Tribune*, Edward Johnson, vice-president of Edison's electric company, used the first electric tree lights on Christmas Eve in 1882. His decoration consisted of 80 hand-blown lights attached to a revolving tree and two strings with 28 more lights hung from the ceiling.

These early lights were not easy to use for the average person. Most houses did not have electricity and the lights were not sold on strings. Each lamp had to be wired individually by an electrician. This process was expensive, and there were not very many qualified "wiremen" at the turn of the century. Thus, electric tree lights were a plaything for the rich to enjoy.

By 1890 General Electric had acquired the rights to Edison's light bulb and major progress toward the illumination of the country began. Prominent citizens, including the President, began to set examples for the rest of the country to follow. According to an article in the *New York Times,* the first Christmas tree lights in the White House appeared in 1895, during the administration of President Cleveland. This was the begininning of a very colorful Christmas tradition at the White House. General Electric continued to experiment with the development of a lamp suitable for the retail market. By 1901 the first lights for the retail trade were advertised. However, these lights still needed to be wired and were not practical since most people still knew nothing about electricity or had the necessary skill to perform the wiring.

The first real breakthrough in the modern lighting revolution came in 1903. An ad in *The Saturday Evening Post* displayed pre-wired lamps called "festoons" or "outfits." These sets were offered for sale by the American Ever-Ready Company and consisted of outfits with 28 sockets using General Electric bulbs and a junction box. The wire was cotton-covered lead; the sockets were brass and porcelain. The lamps were made of various colors of glass. They had carbon filaments, and the exhaust was at the tip. Later strings contained eight series wired lamps, and four of these strings could be attached to one junction box. Energizing the junction box was commonly achieved by screwing the connector from the box into a chandelier socket.

About the same time, the Henry W. McCandless Company of New York introduced similar strings of lights known as Empire Christmas Lights. These lights were pear-shaped, had carbon filaments, and used porcelain sockets and a porcelain junction box. This company merged with Westinghouse in 1914, and the first Westinghouse tree lights appeared in 1915.

Shortly before 1910, imported decorative lights began to appear. Many popular novelty shapes were made by the Kremenetzky Electric Company of Austria. These were carbon filament lamps, in floral or figural shapes made of thin transparent glass. They were handpainted in various colors, and many were coated with crushed glass. By 1910 American made fancy and figural lamps were introduced. During this same year the old pear-shaped bulbs were replaced by round machine-made bulbs.

The first major improvement in the light bulb was the development of the tungsten filament to replace the old and inefficient carbon elements. Although the technology was used in other types of bulbs several years earlier, it was 1916 before General Electric started using these new filaments in Christmas tree lights. These new lights bore the Mazda trademark which the public soon came to recognize as a symbol of superior quality. Other companies soon bought the rights to this technology and began to market their own lights with this trademark also.

The Japanese entered the Christmas bulb market through the courtesy of the Germans and World War I. When the Austrian supply of bulbs was cut off, a prominent importer-Louis Szel-went to Japan to look for a new source of bulbs. There he established an industry which would produce millions of cheap copies of the Austrian bulbs. However, technical problems prevented these copies from approaching the quality of the Austrian lights, and the Japanese soon turned to using white milk glass for their base material. These painted milk glass lights appeared on the American market in 1917. They were imported in great quantities in the succeeding years and are now a familiar sight to many collectors.

The increasing availability of electricity led to a greater popularity of these cheap, and pretty decorations. Many new companies hurried to profit from this growing industry, and faulty strings of lights resulted in an increasing number of tragedies. As a result, safety regulations for tree lights were adopted in 1921. Underwriter Laboratories was instrumental in establishing these safety guidelines, and the public began to demand the Underwriter seal on all tree light strings.

Other basic changes in the bulb itself occurred in the early 1920's. Previously, the evacuation of air from the bulb was accomplished through a small hole in the tip. After the evacuation this hole was sealed by melting it closed with a clear glass rod. Now the evacuation point has been moved to the base. In addition, the shape of the bulb began to change. A cone-shaped light was introduced to replace the round lamps. This new shape proved to be very popular and soon became the mainstay of the industry.

Finally, an invention by Lester Haft of the C.D. Wood

Electric Company made the use of tree lights practical for all Americans with electrical service. A new connector, the "Tachon," or triplug made possible the addition of any number of strings of lights to a tree without the burden of a transformer or junction box. Initially, 15 companies obtained a license to manufacture and market this new connector.

In 1925 these 15 companies formed the National Outfitters Manufacturers' Association (NOMA), and a year later they merged to become the Noma Electric Corporation. In the years which followed, NOMA connectors along with General Electric and Westinghouse lamps became the fundamental decorative lighting systems used in this country. Everything from trees to windows to the entire outsides of houses became the target of eager decorators.

Although strings of parallel lights have been found which can be dated prior to 1920, it was not until the early 1920's that strings of parallel lights began to replace the old series wired strings. The lights on these new strings remined lit when one bulb burned out. This ended the inconvenience of having to test each bulb to find the faulty one. Also, about this time flourescent bulbs began to appear. These were marketed by Westinghouse and Sylvania but did not appeal to the American public and were soon discontinued. As a result, finding examples of these is difficult for the collector today.

A new type of light which was to become the rage of the late 1940's and early 1950's was actually invented in the late 1930's by Carl Otis, who was an accountant for Montgomery Ward. This amatuer inventor developed the principle of the bubble light, which was produced and marketed by NOMA after World War II. The eager public accepted this new light readily, and the NOMA Bubble Lites became the best selling lights ever made. However, it only took a few years until the bubble lights went out of style and faded from the marketplace. Lights and evergreens were replaced by colored floodlights and artificial silver trees in the 1960's.

During the 1970's natural trees and strings of lights made a comeback. However, the new midget lights proved unappealing and troublesome to veteran decorators. To achieve the beauty of fondly remembered holidays, many of the old bubble lights have been returned to the trees. These have been accented with additional decorations consisting of surviving figural and cone-shaped lights. These have been collected and preserved in a wave of nostalgia and are often used in combination with old ornaments to produce trees with unique charm and magic.

Plate 455. Notice the exhaust points at the tips of the early Empire carbon filament bulbs. The set is a 16 socket outfit and has porcelain sockets. Sets like this came in wooden boxes and were sold in the early 1900's.

Plate 456. The light set that came in this box represents one of the earliest examples of multiple lights with a C-7 base. This box is from about 1915 and is marked "Three strands multiple burning Merry Christmas Lights."

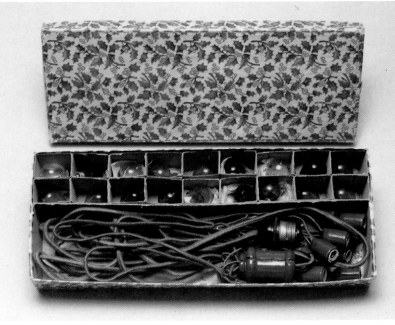

Plate 457. There are two festoons of series lights in this Ever-Ready box. These lamps are carbon filament and were made about 1910.

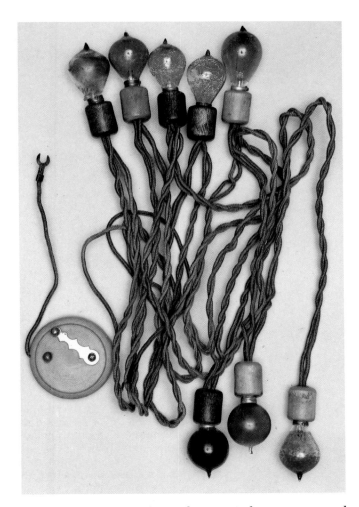

Plate 458. This series' wired string is battery powered. The terminals are hooked to a dry cell. A simple on-off switch is mounted on the round wooden block. The lamps are carbon filament, and the set is from about 1915. Notice most of the colored lights from this period were flashed.

Plate 459. This box of lights was made in England about 1915.

163

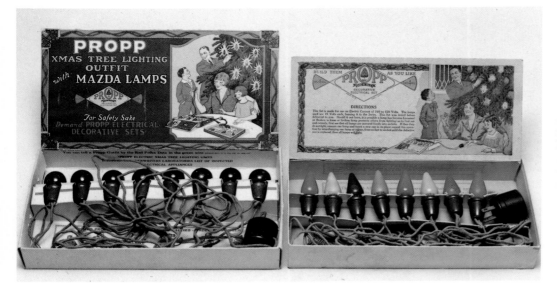

Plate 460. These two boxes contain examples of tree lights made by Propp. The strings have been interchanged and are in the opposite boxes. Copyright dates indicate these sets are from the early 1920's.

Plate 461. This boxed set was made by Zelco. It featured Mazda lamps and probably was made in the early 1920's.

Plate 462. The NRA symbol on the box of this Peerless light set indicates it was a product of the early 1930's. The box bears a 1928 copyright date and states the set is equipped with Japanese lamps.

164

Plate 463. "Luminous candles" were produced by NOMA for both series and parallel strings. This boxed set contains a string of parallel lights which was made in the 1940's.

Plate 464. Tree-top ornaments like this were made by NOMA in the late 1920's and early 1930's.

Plate 465. Flourescent lights are unique in that they have no filaments. Instead they are lighted by passing an electric current through a gas. Ions created by this process cause the phosphorous coating on the bulb to glow. When they are not lit, the color of the lamps is an unimpressive milky white.

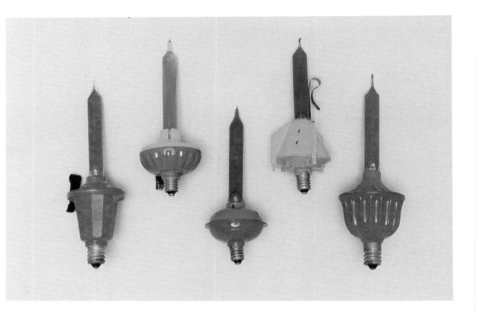

Plate 467 (above) and 468 (below). Bubble lights were introduced in the late 1940's, and some are still being made today. They were made by several different companies and will be found with a number of different base styles. These two photos picture various examples which may be found.

Plate 466. Unlit flourescent lights may be easily overlooked by novice collectors.

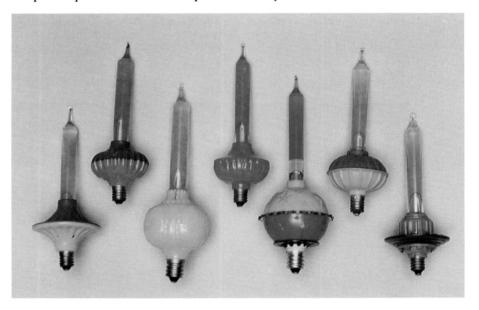

Plate 469. Kristal Star lamps are star-like glass lamps. The set consists of ten lamps 2½" in diameter, which were made in Japan.

Plate 470. Matchless lights came in different sizes and with different types of bases. The lights pictured here have standard, intermediate, and series type bases. These lights all have glass prisms, but some were also made with plastic prisms. Notice the tree lights shown with frosted prisms. These are scarce. The three sizes pictured are 2", 2½", and 3" in diameter. These lights were made in the 1930's and were sold by the Matchless Company of Chicago.

Plate 471. These lights are all early European with the exception of the cat (top right) which was made in Japan during the early 1920's. Top: Clown, Angel, Cat with spectacles. Bottom: Snowman with club, Dwarf with shovel, Horn player.

Plate 472. These are all early German Father Christmas lamps. The large one measures 6", and the others are between 3" and 3¼" long. The presence of the prominent exhaust tip at the top of most of these indicates they were made prior to 1920.

167

Plate 473. These figural lights are very early. They were made in Germany and paper was used as the insulator. The jester head on the left is 3" high, the Indian is 3¾" long, and the clown head is 3" long.

Plate 474. These five heads are of English origin. They are marked "Foreign" on the base. The head on the top left is the "king head," the one on the top right is an Indian chief, and the one on the bottom right is a pig. The other two heads are possible Howdy-Doody types. Each head is 2½" long.

Plate 475. Left: Jester pointing to a playing card. Center: Dutch girl. Right: Snowman on skis.

Plate 476. Top row: a. Little girl with a camera in a red dress; b. Little girl with a camera in a green dress; c. Little girl with a muff; d. Baby in a red dress. Bottom row: a. Little aviator; b. Little boy in a green shirt; c. Baby in a red sock.

Plate 477. These lights are part of a series produced from the 1930's to the 1950's. The lights represent characters from popular comic strips. Top row: a. Dick Tracy; b. Betty Boop; c. Little Orphan Annie; d. Moon Mullins. Bottom row: a. Andy Gump; b. Smitty; c. Peewee.

Plate 478. Top: red and blonde hair girl heads. Bottom: a. Kewpie doll; b. Little girl in a rose; c. Angel; d. Child in a Christmas suit.

Plate 479. Left to right: a. Little Boy Blue; b. Mother Goose; c. Humpty Dumpty (bust); d. Humpty Dumpty (full-figure).

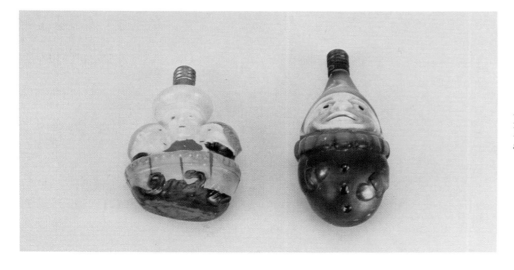

Plate 480. Left: Three men in a tub. Right: Clown with a red ruffled collar and blue suit.

170

Plate 481. The lights in this photo are in the very rare category. Top: Jackie Coogan, Canadian Mountie, Betty Boop. Bottom: Dog in a clown suit, Flapper girl, Chinese schoolgirl.

Plate 482. Top: a. Clown head with ruffled yellow collar; b. Clown head with wide smile. Bottom: a. Clown with a mask; b. Chubby clown in polka-dot suit.

Plate 483. Top: a. Large snowman with a stick, 4"; b. Small snowman with a stick, 2¼"; c. Snowman in three button suit. Bottom: a. Roly-poly snowman with a red hat; b. Roly-poly snowman with a black hat; c. Snowman holding an umbrella.

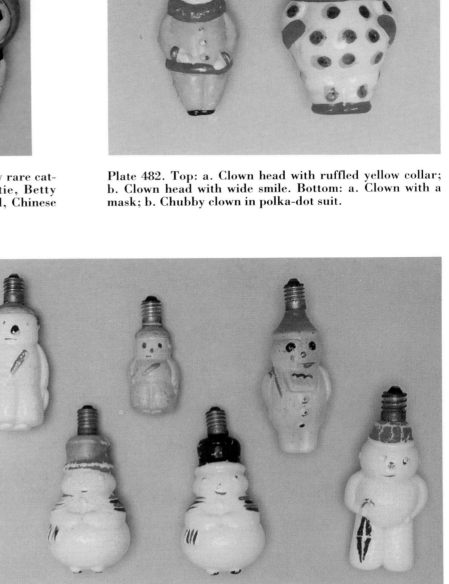

Plate 484. These painted milk glass Santa lights are a nice addition to a collection. The lights are fairly large at 3½" to 4" in length. The two flat oval-shaped lights on the right are called "Santa Scenes."

Plate 485. Painted white milk glass Japanese Santa figures are among the most commonly found lamps. The heads in this picture are 2" to 2¾" long, and the full-figures are about 3½" long.

Plate 486. Top: a. Hunch-back Santa with large yellow bag; b. Father Christmas in long robe; c. Mazda Santa. Bottom: a. Santa face on yellow chimney; b. Santa face on green chimney; c. Santa face on a red chimney; d. Standing Santa.

Plate 487. This photo shows some of the more commonly found bells with an embossed Santa face. Notice the original price tag on the bell in the lower left corner.

Plate 488. Left: Standing Santa figure with a large green bag. Center: Large Santa head on a chimney. Right: Three faced Santa head.

Plate 489. Obtaining the animal figures shown here will be of moderate difficulty for the average collector. Top: Golfing rooster, Duck, Clown dog, Cat holding ball. Center: Dog in polo outfit, Chick, Horse in a horseshoe. Bottom: Frog, Squirrel, Dismal Desmond, Mother cat with a baby in a basket.

Plate 490. Top: a. Seated reindeer; b. Elephant with a long trunk. Bottom: a. Horse head in a horseshoe; b. Seated pink panther.

174

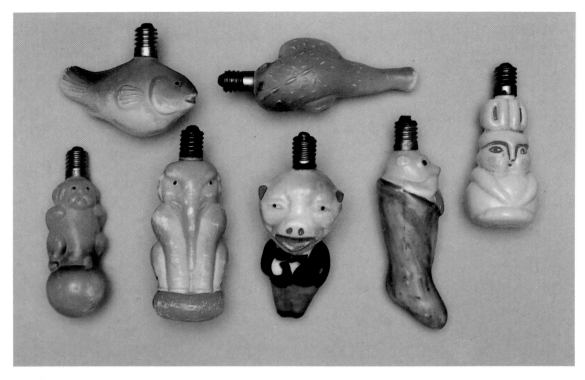

Plate 491. Animals were favorite subjects of tree light designers. Many times these characters were depicted in an interesting or unusual manner. Top: Fish, Tadpole. Bottom: Dog on a ball, Pink elephant, Pig in a suit, Dog in a sock, Rabbit.

Plate 492. Left to right: a. Begging cat; b. Puffed-up cat; c. Cat with a banjo; d. Red seated scotty; e. Two monkeys in a shoe; f. Bulldog on a ball.

Plate 493. These are interesting Japanese animal lamps. The figures are painted over white milk glass and are sometimes hard-to-find with good paint. Top: Scotty with baby, Owl with vest, Cat with apron, Hippo. Bottom: Round frog (rare), Nesting dove, Pig with horn, Pig with drum.

Plate 494. These figural lights were made in Japan between the 1920's and the 1950's. Top: Owl, Cat, Sitting dog, Wolf head. Bottom: Pink bear, Peacock, Burro.

Plate 495. With the exception of the blue teddy bear, these are some of the more commonly found Japanese animals. Top: Blue teddy bear, Bartender bulldog, Bear strumming a banjo. Bottom: Kitten, Lion with a tennis racquet, Cat in an evening dress, Lion with a pipe.

Plate 496. These lamps are early European animals. The two birds were probably made before 1900. The insulator on one is ivory, and the other has a plaster insulator. The glass figural part of the lion was made in Europe, but the light part is Mazda. All the lamps are about 3" long. Top: Cat, Lion, Owl, Monkey. Bottom: Bird, Bird, Monkey.

Plate 497. Common songbirds in decorated white milk glass are among the most frequently seen lights. The socket is normally found on the bird's back. Most of these lights were made from the 1930's to the 1950's.

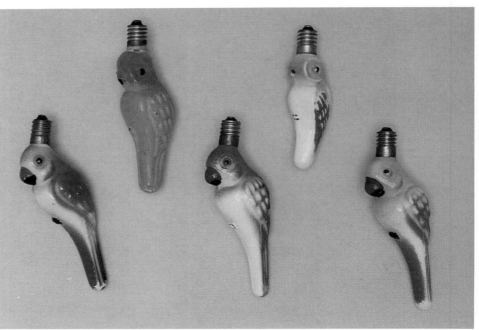

Plate 498. Decorated white milk glass parrots and parakeets are commonly found lights. These were made in Japan from the 1930's through the 1950's.

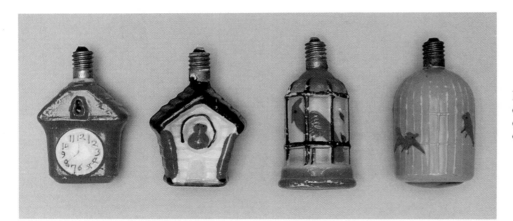

Plate 499. Left to right: a. Cuckoo clock; b. Bird in a house-shaped cage; c. Red bird in a cage; d. Red birds embossed on a bright yellow cage.

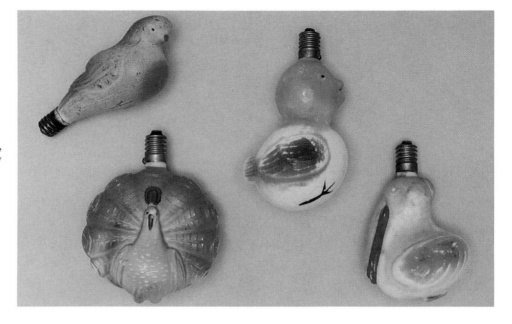

Plate 500. Left to right: a. Early bird, decorated on clear glass; b. Brightly colored peacock; c. Chick; d. Pelican.

These European birds have exhaust tips at their beaks. They are 3¼" to 4½" long. The bird on the top right with the long tubular base was made as a shell. It had a Mazda lamp inserted later.

Plate 502. These European fruits are examples of lights made between 1910 and 1930. The grapes, lemon, and peach, are early. The walnut has an ivory insulator, which is uncommon.

Plate 503. Top row: a. Pineapple; b. Purple grape cluster; c. Apple; d. Fruit cluster. Bottom row: a. Green grape culster; b. Large fruit basket; c. Yellow grape cluster.

Plate 504. Decorated white milk glass flowers such as these pictured are commonly found lights. These were made in Japan from the 1930's through the 1950's.

Plate 505. This hard-to-find light is a flower in a seashell. It is about 2¾" long.

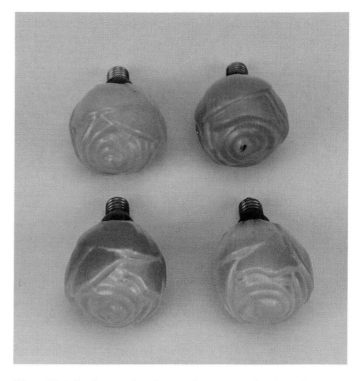

Plate 506. Lights in the shape of roses can be found in various colors, 2½" long.

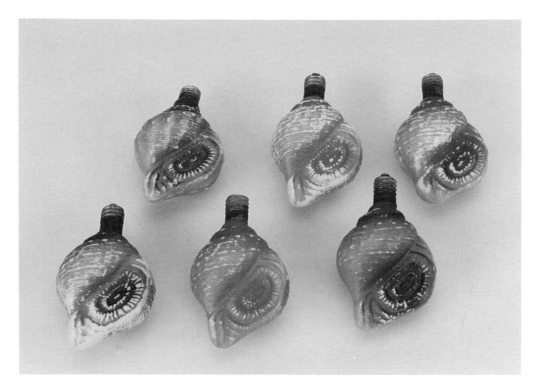

Plate 507. These colorful lights are shaped like seashells. They are 3" long and can be found in several colors.

Plate 508. Decorated white milk glass lights in the shape of snow-covered houses are frequently seen. These lights were made in Japan from the 1930's through the 1950's.

Plate 509. Lanterns are commonly found Christmas tree lights. They are attractive decorations since they were made in many different shapes and sizes.

Plate 510. These lamps and lanterns are relatively easy to find. They were made in Japan from the mid 1920's through the 1950's.

Plate 511. Common lanterns are abundant and still inexpensive enough to appeal to the beginning collector.

Plate 512. Left to right: a. Hunter stalking a deer; b. Santa coming to the door; c-d. Santa in a sleigh being pulled by a reindeer.

Plate 513. When they are used to decorate a tree, lights in the shape of stars, decorated balls, or other interesting shapes add a charming look to a collection of lights

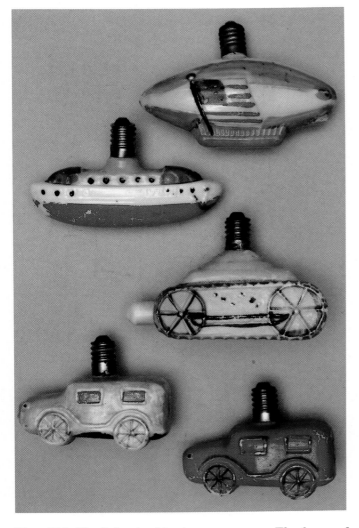

Plate 515. Silvered ornament lights with indents were imported from Japan in the mid-1930's. Some will be found without indents, and other shapes were made. None of these lights are easy to find.

Plate 514. The lights in this picture are rare. The forms of transportation shown are from the top: a Zepplin, a ship, a tank, and two autos.

Plate 516. These lights are called miniatures. Miniatures include lights up to 1½" in length. The lights were made in Japan from the 1930's to the 1950's. The most common miniatures are parrots and Santas. Top: Pink snowman, Dog on a ball, Parrot, Pink teddy bear. Center: Indian head, White snowman, Kewpie, Santa. Bottom: Hound dog head, Santa head, Bulldog, Rabbit with walking stick.

Plate 517. These miniature lights are all under 1½" long. All the lights pictured here are Japanese with the exception of the clear grape in the bottom right which is European. Top: Flower, Beach ball, House. Center: Drum, Grapes, Lantern. Bottom: Auto, Lantern, Clear grape.

Plate 518. Some of the more commonly found shapes of miniature lights are lamps, lanterns and fruits.

185

Plate 519. Ten different lights are included in this nursery rhyme set. Each light is about 3" long. Top: Sing a Song of Sixpence, The Cow Jumped over the Moon, The Cat and the Fiddle, Humpty Dumpty, Little Red Riding Hood. Bottom: Little boy Blue, Ole King Cole, Little Jack Horner, Mother Goose, Jack and Jill.

Plate 520. This nursery rhyme set, smaller than the one previously shown, was made in the 1940's and 1950's. The five lights pictured are Jack and Jill, The Old Woman in a Shoe, Mother Hubbard, Little Jack Horner, and Mother Goose.

186

Plate 521. This set of Walt Disney character lights was unauthorized and was only produced for a short time. They have the small C-6 base for use in series strings, and the characters are a little smaller than the ones below which were produced later. Top: Pinocchio, Dwarf, Mickey Mouse. Bottom: Donald Duck, Fiddler Pig, Minnie Mouse, Pluto.

Plate 522. In the 1960's Paramount obtained a license from Disney to produce this set of eight characters. These are larger than the lights above. They are molded a little more crudely, and have a C-7 base for use in parallel strings. Top: Jiminy Cricket, Pinocchio, Minnie Mouse, Mickey Mouse. Bottom: Dwarf, Donald Duck, Pluto, Fiddler Pig.

Plate 523. This set of shades was produced by NOMA and was introduced at the New York World's Fair in 1939. The shades were illuminated by a regular C-6 Mazda lamp.

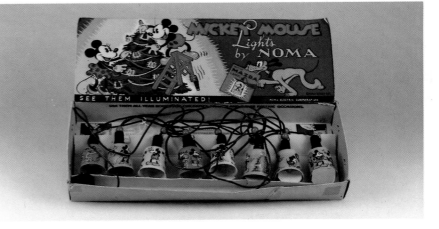

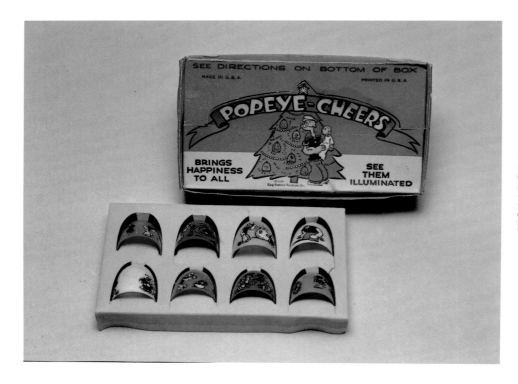

Plate 524. "Popeye Cheers" was a set of shades produced by the Royal Electric company of Pawtucket, Rhode Island. These shades have a copyright date of 1929. They were designed to be hung over bulbs for illumination.

Plate 525. These revolving shades were made by the Sail-Me Co. of Chicago. There are two parts to each ornament. The small cone-shaped piece with the needle is placed over a regular cone-type bulb. The colored shades are then balanced on the needle. Heat from the lights causes air currents which cause the shades to revolve.

Plate 526. Cardboard houses with lamps were imported from Japan during the 1930's. They had colored cellophane on their windows and doors for the light to shine through. The mark on the bottom is "Nippon Registration No. 71613."

Plate 527. These lights were made in England in the 1920's and early 1930's. They are 3" long and are marked "Foreign" on the base. The figures are from left: Santa Claus, Dog, Pot of flowers, and Cat.

Plate 528. These American miniature figurals were developed at the General Electric research facility in Nela Park, OH but were never put into production. Left to right: Dog, Squirrel, Rabbit, Pig.

Plate 529. Multi-colored plastic Mirostar reflectors were produced by the NOMA Electric Corporation. They could be used with either C-6 or C-7½ lamps "to intensify the light from Christmas tree lights several times over."

Decorations Around and Under the Christmas Tree
Christmas Tree Stands

Early German trees were of the table-top variety, and most were nailed to flat boards of cross-shaped supports. Later, with the use of larger trees, especially in the United States, a more sturdy support was needed.

At first, these larger trees were merely replanted in dirt-filled crocks or large wooden boxes. These primitive supports were usually covered with paper or other decorative material.

After the Civil War various types of tree stands, which were designed to hold large sizes of cut evergreens, were patented. These designs were variations of cast iron three-legged stands. Most early stands had features which allowed them to be attached to the floor for additional support.

In the 1870's a key-wound musical tree stand was invented. When the spring mechanism was wound up, the tree would revolve, and a music box in the base played a popular Christmas tune.

By the beginning of the 1900's the first tree stands with cups to hold water for the tree began to appear. These early stands were expensive and were not affordable for the average family of that era. However, by the end of WWI many trees were staying fresh longer thanks to these new water-holding stands.

In the 1920's tree stands with lights for the purpose of illuminating the base of the tree began to appear. Later, as tree lights became more popular, plugs were added to the stands, so the lights could be plugged directly into the stands. Some of the lighted stands were very elaborate. They were decorated in the colors of the season and usually had a water reservoir. One of the more advanced models even had the ability to revolve.

Through the 1940's three-footed metal stands with water reservoirs were common. In the late fifties and during the sixties revolving stands were popular again. Most of these later stands were musical, and many were designed to hold artificial trees. The latest designs for cut evergreens are usually red and green three-footed tin stands with some type of water reservoir. Most of these are not as sturdy as their predecessors, and many trees tend to topple with the slightest jolt.

A few examples of the various styles of tree stands manufactured from the late nineteenth century to the mid-twentieth century are pictured.

Plate 530. This is a key wind-up musical stand which also rotates the tree. It is 15" in diameter and has a metal top fastened to a wooden base.

Plate 531. This fancy tree stand is made of cast iron. Scenes on the base include children watching a clown, children with Santa, a church with a shining star, and a house on a hillside with a large tree. The base is 11" square. The tree stand on the right is designed to hold a feather tree. It is a musical stand which was made in Switzerland, and it is 8" in diameter and 5½" high.

Plate 532. This key wind-up musical tree stand is not as large as the one in Plate 530. It is only 11" in diameter.

Plate 533. This fancy tree stand features a manger scene at the base of the tree. It has a key wind-up music box and uses an electric motor to rotate the tree.

Plate 534. This Santa Claus head is a heavy concrete tree stand. It is 11½" high and sturdy enough to hold just about any tree.

Plate 535. This light-up tree stand dates back to the 1920's. One very similar to this may be found in early Noma Electric Corporation ads. It had a decorative snowy base studded with lamps which were intended to light the base of the tree.

Plate 536. This metal tree stand was sold by the Noma Electric Company in the forties. It has eight series lamps and features an add-on plug. The metal pot in the center was designed to hold water to help keep the tree fresh.

Plate 537. This metal stand conceals a motor which enables the tree to rotate. The stand is about 15" square.

Fences

For many years it has been popular to use fences made of cast iron, wood, or tin to encircle the Christmas tree.

Early wooden fences were often homemade. Commercial versions of fences were often sold in sections which had to be assembled. Depending on the type of fence, sections usually ranged from fifteen to twenty-four inches in length. One or two gates were included with each fence.

Fences were constructed in various sizes and shapes, including squares, rectangles, circles, and diamonds.

Wooden and cast iron fences have been found in advertisements as early as the late 1800's. In the 1920's the Noma Electric Company offerred a wooden fence with lighted fence posts. These continued to be popular through the forties. Goose-feather hedge-type fences complete with red composition berry post tips were offered in the 1930's. In the 1940's and 1950's red and green wooden fences were popular. These were made in many shapes and sizes by a variety of manufacturers.

Although the older and more elaborate fences are more valuable and prized by collectors, many people are also seeking the newer green and red fences to use with their holiday decorations. The following pages illustrate some of the types of fences which may be found.

Plates 538 & 539. This is a dyed goose-feather hedge row fence with red composition berries. The complete fence consists of ten regular sections and one gate section. Each section is approximately 3" high and 10" long. The completed fence is about twenty inches square. This type of fence was sold by such companies as Sears and Montgomery Ward in the early 1930's.

Plate 540. The wicker sections of this fence slip over red wooden posts for support. The wicker sections are 12" long and 5½" high. The entire fence produces a square about twenty-four inches in size. The tin bases of the posts are marked: "A.W. DRAKE MFG. CO. HAZELTON, PA. PATD."

Plate 541. This is a nice early walnut fence designed to have a Victorian look. Each section is 15" long and 6" high. The whole fence encloses a square of about thirty inches. A single gate about five inches wide is included.

Plate 542. This green and white fence from the 1920's has both a front and rear gate. The entire fence is very large. It consists of six sections which are 18" long and 8" high.

194

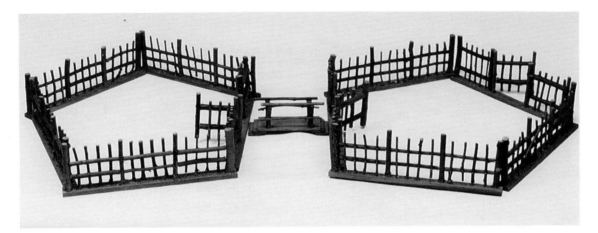

Plate 543. There are two five-sided enclosed areas and a connecting bridge to this log fence. There are two gates in both sections of the fence.

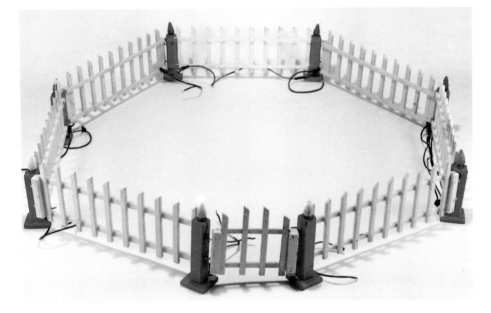

Plate 544. This elaborate fence was advertised by the Noma Electric Corporation as early as the mid 1920's. There were eight sections which formed an eight-sided fence. The red support posts contained bulbs which were wired together in series. Each section is about 14" long and 6" high. One gate is included which is six inches wide.

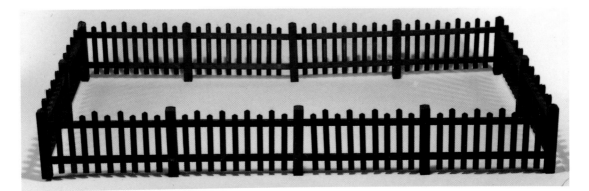

Plate 545. Fences which were built to be used on trees which set on the floor were often very large, as this one is. This green wooden fence includes 12 sections. Each section is 22" long and 7" high.

Plate 546. An unusual diamond shape is produced by this log rail fence. The log sections are held together by wire clips. Each section is 12" long, and the fence is 6" high. There is a single gate section which is 6" wide.

Plate 547. Red and green tin wire fences were very popular and may be found in many sizes. The small sizes were usually table-top fences and were often used around small feather trees. The larger sizes were used on the floor around a full-size evergreen. The sections of this fence are 10" long and 6" high. This completed fence produces a square of twenty inches. The gate is two-parts and is 6" wide.

Plate 548. This white wooden fence is built on a raised wooden platform set on legs about 3" high. The fence encloses an area about 22" square.

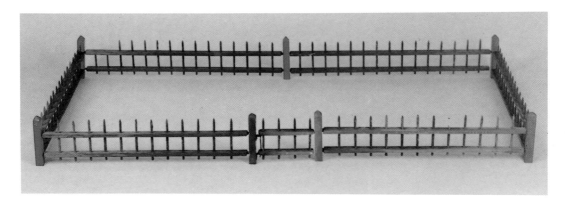

Plate 549. The vertical posts of this green and red wooden fence are made of sharply pointed round dowels. The fence is very large and was possibly home-made. It consists of 6 sections, each 22" long, and has a single gate.

196

Plate 550. Small hinges connect the sections of this green and red wooden fence. The fence produces and enclosure 18" square. There is a single gate which is connected to the fence by hinges.

Plate 551. The posts and fancy gate lend an elegant look to this simple red and green wooden fence. The sections are 4" high and produce an enclosure 18" square.

Plate 552. The Valley Novelty Works of Bloomsburg, PA manufactured this flat rail wooden fence. It has a single gate, is 4½" high, and encloses an area 18" square.

197

Nativity Scenes – Villages – Animals

The tradition of placing such items as nativity scenes, villages, and animals under the Christmas tree has probably been adopted from the old German custom of having a Putz scene beneath the tree. The central theme of the Putz was the nativity scene with its assortment of figures and animals. Over the years the Putz scenes became more elaborate, and whole villages began to appear under the tree. Today, the idea has been expanded to include other items such as miniature trains and their associated towns, villages, and scenery.

Nativity scenes have been made from many materials. Some of the more elaborate ones are made of wood or china, but numerous sets composed of paper or cardboard will be found. Figures and animals were made of wood, composition, plaster, celluloid, and cardboard. The most commonly found village pieces are made of cardboard coated with mica. However, wood was also used, and McLoughlin Brothers produced a village of chromolithiographed cardboard in the late 1800's.

Plate 553. The animals, Mary, Joseph, the Christ Child, and the Three Wise Men are common figures for a Putz scene. These figures are made of plaster, and the stable is made of wood.

Plate 554. A variety of animals were popular, including sheep, cows, donkeys, horses and camels. These figures are made of plaster, and the stable is made of wood.

Plate 555. Lithographed cardboard manger sets were popular during the 1950's. This set was made in the United States by Concordia.

Plate 556. Some Japanese mica-covered village pieces were elaborate. These two pieces have cotton covered roofs to simulate snow. Height: left, 10"; right, 14".

Plate 557. Coated cardboard village pieces. Made in Japan, 5" to 6" high.

Plate 558. Coated cardboard village pieces from Japan, 4" to 5" high.

Plate 559. The doors and windows of these small Japanese coated cardboard village pieces are covered with colored cellophane and lights can be inserted through small holes in the back, 3" to 5" high.

200

Plate 560. These coated cardboard houses were made in Japan. They are more detailed than most Japanese village pieces. Height: front, 3½"; rear, 5½" to 6½".

Plate 561. These village pieces are coated with mica. Wooden village pieces are not as common as cardboard pieces. Left: House, 4½" high, 6" long, 6" wide. Center: Railroad station, 4½" high, 4" long, 2½" wide. Right: Schoolhouse, 4½" high, 4" long, 2½" wide.

Plate 562. These small village pieces are coated with mica and decorated with small colored balls.

Plate 563. These German sheep are from the early 1900's. Their ribbon collars are marked "Germany," 5" high.

Plate 564. A rare early 1900's German black sheep is shown here. The collars are marked "Germany," 3" to 3½" high.

Plate 565. Boxed set of early 1900's sheep and shepherd, 2" to 2½" high.

Plate 566. Spotted sheep are not easily found. These were made in Germany, 2½" high.

Plate 567. Compostion reindeer and sleigh. The reindeer are 3" long; the sleigh is 6" long.

Plate 568. Early reindeer were often made of papier-mache. These papier-mache reindeer are 3" long. The sled is mica coated cardboard. It is marked "Germany" and is 3" long.

Plate 569. Reindeer are commonly associated with Christmas and are often placed under the tree. These are small metal reindeer from the early 1900's, 2" high.

Bisque Figures

Miniature china figures were made in Germany and Japan during the 1920's and 1930's. Many of these figures were miniature child-like figures covered with snow. These are referred to as snow babies. German figures have excellent color and detail, while many of the Japanese figures are of poorer quality. Most snow babies are between 1½" and 3½" high.

Other miniature china figures were also made. Some juvenile china face figures, called snow children, had brightly colored paper or cotton clothes. Miniature Santa figures were also made of bisque. Both German and Japanese figures will be found. Japanese figures usually lack the fine detail of their German counterparts.

Plate 570. This tree ornament has a bisque face and arms. Her dress is cotton, 4" high.

Plate 571. Snow babies on sleds. German. Left: Wooden sled with snow baby pulled by two snowbears, 7" long. Right: Snow baby on wooden sled, 3¼" long.

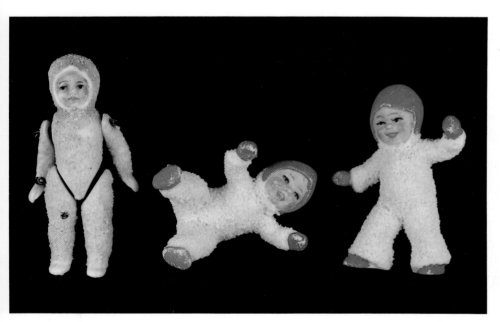

Plate 572. German snow babies. Jointed babies like the one on the left are not easy to find. It is 3½" tall. The other two are nicely painted. They are 2½" high.

Plate 573. These merry little snow children were made in Germany. Their detail is exceptional, 2½" high.

Plate 574. Snow children on skis add charm to these planters, 4½" high.

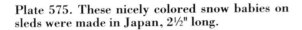

Plate 575. These nicely colored snow babies on sleds were made in Japan, 2½" long.

Plate 576. Snow babies and snow bears at play. Figures are German with the possible exception of the snowman on the left, which could be Japanese.

Plate 577. Japanese snow babies and snow bear. Figures are 1¼" to 1¾" high.

Plate 578. Miniature bisque Santa figures, 2" to 3½" high.

Plate 579. Left: Santa on a sled, 3" long. Center: Santa on a sleigh pulled by a reindeer with its horns missing, 3¼" long. Right: Santa pulled by a horse, marked "Germany," 2¾" long.

Plate 580. Variety of miniature bisque German and Japanese Santa figures, 1½" to 2¾" high.

Plate 581. Miniature china Santa figures going down the chimney of snow-covered houses. Left, 2½"; Right, 3".

207

Plate 582. Left: China Santa with large green open bag for candy canes, 6" high. Right: China Santa nodder, marked "Germany," 3¼" high.

Plate 583. Left: Small china Santa figure, 2¼" high. Right: Ornate miniature china Santa with large green sack, 3½" high.

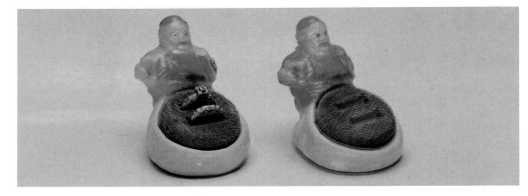

Plate 584. Santa figural ring holder, 3½" high.

Plate 585. Miniature elf-like candle holders were made in both Germany and Japan. They measure ¾" to 1¼" high.

Cake Tins and Candy Containers

From the earliest days of the Christmas festival, candy, cookies, and other edibles have been favorite gifts for the children. As a result, a great number of containers to hold these sweets have been designed. They range from the very elaborate and expensive papier-mache figurals produced in the nineteenth century to the simple and inexpensive boxes made in the 1940's and 1950's.

Candy containers can be found made of almost any material – paper, cardboard, plastic, glass, tin, or cloth. Most were designed to hang from the family Christmas tree long after their tasty contents had been eagerly devoured. As fragile as most of these containers were, many of them have survived the perils of time and are now being enjoyed by avid collectors.

Many of these containers were very easy to make. Therefore, they were made at home in great quatities. Most women's magazines in the early 1900's even contained instructions for making cornucopias, baskets, and other items of simple design. Many times these homemade crafts were decorated with scraps or tinsel. These pieces added much charm to the trees and gave the novice craftsman a warm feeling of accomplishment.

Adding to the abundance of the homemade products were the hundreds of examples of simple candy containers available from commercial sources at reasonable prices. For example, wholesale prices of cornucopias and boxes were often less than two dollars per hundred in the years before World War I.

During the 1930's Japan became the major supplier of small, cheap candy containers. Many of these pieces feature a Santa figure with a fabric net body and a celluloid face. Also, a lot of Santa figures are often found in a basket, boot, shoe, or going down a chimney.

Many collectors today are seeking the larger more desirable papier-mache figures which were made around the turn of the century. These include belsnickles, Father Christmas figures, animals, and snowmen. Some of these pieces had removable heads, while others had thin paper seals which were designed to be broken. These pieces, when found in good condition, are commanding exhorbitant prices.

The following pages contain some examples of candy containers. For other candy containers see the Santa Claus and paper ornament sections of this book.

Plate 586. Snow White and the Seven Dwarfs are posing as candy containers. Snow White is 6" high, and the Dwarfs are 5" high. The figures are made of papier-mache, and they are marked "W.D. PROD. MADE IN GERMANY."

Plate 587. During the 1920's and 1930's children often received their Christmas candy in containers like these. The sleds in the front row are cardboard with a mica coating. The little corn husk cup with the scrap angel on the side was a nut container. All these containers are 3" to 4" high. The shoe with the baby head container is made of cardboard covered with cloth.

Plate 588. Pictured are four examples of Japanese candy containers, which were produced in great quantities from the twenties through the 1950's. The boot on the left is made of chenille. It is 4" high and has a net mesh top with a drawstring opening. The standing Santa candy container has a celluloid face and a fabric net torso. He is 7" high. The red net candy container is 7" long. He has a celluloid face, hands, and boots. The wholesale price for containers of this type in the mid 1920's was $8.40 a gross. The Santa on the wicker basket has a celluloid face and is 4" high.

Plate 589. These candy containers were made in Japan after 1920. The boot on the left is 6" high, is foil covered, and has chenille trim. The Santa has a plaster face which is a little unusual for containers of this era. The white net container in the center is 7" long. The Santa head is made of celluloid. The basket on the right is made of chenille and is topped with a fabric net containing a celluloid Santa head. This container is 4" high.

Plate 590. This boot candy container was made in Japan. It is 7" high and is topped by a Santa with a plaster face and a cotton beard.

Plate 591. Little baskets with drawstring net closures were popular Christmas candy containers. The Santa face is celluloid.

Plate 592. Left: Santa horn candy container with mesh drawstring top, 4" long. Center: Net mesh Santa candy container with celluloid face, clay hands and feet, 6" high. Right: Santa at the chimney candy container. The candy which once filled the container was made by Candy Crafters, Inc. of Lansdowne, PA.

Plate 593. Mica coated cardboard candy container in the shape of roly-poly Santa. It has a composition face and a rabbit fur beard. 10½" high; 6" in diameter.

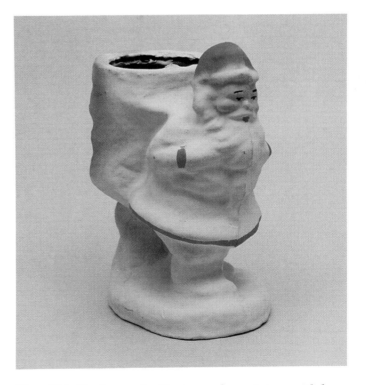

Plate 594. Papier-mache Santa candy container with large bag, 8" high.

Plate 595. Left: Papier-mache Santa candy container with a net bag. Right: Santa riding a bear candy container, papier-mache, 6½" high.

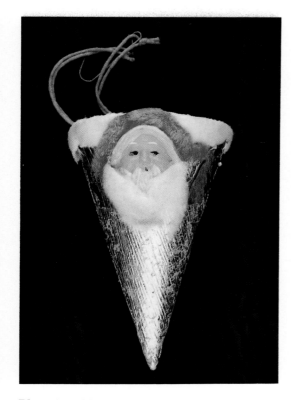

Plate 596. Many cornucopia style candy containers were made of foil. This one features a celluloid Santa head.

Plate 597. Chenille boots with removable tops often doubled as candy containers and tree ornaments. The boot with the holly is 6" high, and the one with the plaster Santa head is 7" high. Both were made in Japan.

Plate 598. Boot candy containers are frequently found. There are different styles and many will be decorated with a Santa head.

Plate 599. This snowman candy container is 9" tall and is marked "Made in Germany." It is made of mica-coated cardboard and has a cotton batting carrot nose.

Plate 600. Left: Snowman playing accordion candy container, 5" high. Right: Candy container with Santa figure, marked "Made in Western Germany," 3¾" high.

Plate 601. German mica-covered snowmen were often candy containers. This snowman with a black top hat, cane and carrot-type nose is 6" high.

Plate 602. These figures are all candy containers. The two Santas have torsos which lift off their legs to reveal their hidden compartment. The figure on the left is Japanese. He has a plaster face and a cotton coat and is 7" high. The Santa in the center is 9" high. He has a cotton coat, plaster face, and is marked "Selfredge, London." The figure on the right is a 7" high papier-mache snowman with a feather tree and a cotton batting carrot nose.

Plate 603. The two containers in this photo have heads which are attached with springs. The snowman is made of coated cardboard and is 7" high. The figure on the left is made of felt over red cardboard. It is 13" high and is marked "Container made in Germany."

Plate 604. The small goose-feather tree above has a holly decorated flower pot base which is a candy container. The tree has spring-type candle clips and is 6" high.

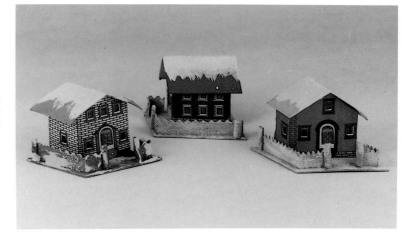

Plate 605. Cardboard houses were sometimes made in the form of candy containers. The roof of each house lifts off to reveal the hidden goodies. The houses are about 6" high and 6" square.

Plate 606. Painted glass containers were also used to sell candy. One of the more common glass containers is on the left. It is in the shape of a chimney, and Santa with a large bag is starting down the chimney. The container on the right has Santa riding a rocking horse.

Plate 607. Jolly Santa figures often appeared on a cardboard box style candy containers. The box on the left measures 10½" x 6¼" x 1¾", and the one on the right is 10¾" high by 1¾" deep.

Plate 608. These thin cardboard candy containers are similar to the types produced from the 1930's through the 1950's. The Santa face is 4" in diameter. The two boxes on the bottom are rectangular – about 2" deep, 3" high, and 4" long. The "Huyler's' box is 2½" deep, 4¾" long, and 5½" high.

Plate 609. Front left: The Hind Co., Pittsburg, PA. 3" x6", cardboard. Front center: Cardboard box with girl holding a cat. 2¼" x 3¼". Front right: Holly decorated heart tin, 5" diameter. Rear left: Tin box with Santa bust, 4" diameter. Rear center: Stetson hat box. Oval shape, 3¾" x 4¼". This small-size sample was given as a symbol of the gift, and the recipient then went to the store to be fitted for the real hat. Rear right: Norweigian Anchovies, Frederickstadt Preserving Co., Fredreckstadt, Norway. An 8-sided tin.

Plate 610. Front left: 5" x 8" rectangular tin with five different 1920's winter scenes. Front center: Jacob's Biscuits, "Christmas Cake for Children." Front right: 8-sided tin by Horner, 4" x 5". Rear left: Mackintosh Christmas Festival Chocolate Assortment. Rear right: 8-sided tin with lady on skis, 9½" diameter.

Plate 611. Front left: Rountree's Cocoa Works, York, England. Front center: Jacob's Biscuits "Christmas Cake for Children." Front right: Henry Vincent, Ltd., Worcestorshire, England. "Take the Home Sweet Home," Blue Bird Toffee. Center: CWS Biscuits, Crumpsall & Cardiff. Rear left: Carol Honor Candies, Buffalo-Cleveland. Rear right: Huntley and Palmer.

Plate 612. Christmas tins with handles were often given to children. They could be used later as a lunch pail. The oval tin pictures Santa landing on the rooftop in an airplane.

Plate 613. Pictured is an oval Christmas tin decorated with holly and snowmen which once held Madison mixed hard candy.

217

Paper Christmas Items
Chromos – Die-cuts – Scraps

The invention of chromolithograpy in the mid 1800's had a profound influence on the manner in which the Christmas tree was decorated in the last half of the nineteenth century. This new printing process was invented in England and was perfected in Germany. The industrious German printers exploited this new process to its fullest. They produced millions of cheap prints which were eagerly gobbled up by a picture-starved population.

The printing process was very painstaking. As many as 20 colors were used on each print, and each color had to be printed separately. After printing the pieces were embossed to produce a three dimensional appearance. This process produced excellent quality, full-color reproductions of many of the figures associated with Christmas. Many of the favorite subjects were German Santas, cherubs, angels, snowmen, children, and Christmas trees. The smallest were just over an inch high while the largest could reach eighteen inches. The individual prints were cut out by dies. They came in large sheets and were joined together by small tabs. This process of cutting out the prints by machine with the use of dies has resulted in their being commonly called "die-cuts."

Die-cuts came both as full-figures and partial-figures. The full figures were often used to decorate the tops of cookies. They were either glued to the cookie or attached with frosting. These decorated cookies were then placed on the tree for decoration. After Christmas many of these cookies were eaten. However, some of them were dried and used as decorations for many years.

Partial-figure die-cuts were used in combination with other materials to produce ornaments. Some of the more popular ornaments combined die-cuts with spun glass or tinsel. Many cotton figural ornaments may also be found with these colorful paper faces, hands, or feet.

Around the turn of the century printers began producing die-cuts with mirror-image reverse sides. The two pieces were then glued together to make a genuine double-sided ornament.

Each Christmas season new sets of die-cuts appeared on the market. The decorations became very elaborate, and the scope of designs produced was only limited by the imagination of the printers. In addition to using these colorful prints on the Christmas tree, many people kept large numbers of them in scrapbooks. A scrapbook craze swept the country in the last half of the nineteenth century, and choice die-cuts were sought after in much the same manner as they are today. This form of collection resulted in the term "scraps," a name by which these chromolithographed prints are still referred to today.

Many large stand-up paper items were made of pressed paper and lacked much of the fine detail of the earlier die-cuts. Most of these pieces are embossed. Some fold out. Many are covered with glitter. Some of the more popular figures were Santas, nativity scenes, and Santa in a sleigh pulled by reindeer.

Many die-cuts are still being made today. These items usually show up for sale at the flea markets a few months before Christmas every year. Many of these new ones are double-sided and are very thin. Collectors look for sharply printed features, deep embossing, a thick paper or cardboard backing, and obvious signs of age such as wear or yellowing of the backing to help them distinguish old scraps from the new ones.

Plate 614. This combination of various sized Father Christmas figures and heads are all German with the exception of the one in the white robe. That one is marked "E. Heller, Made in Austria." Notice, also, the partial figure in the blue coat. The tree is 4½" high and the heads are 1½" to 2" high. The other figures are 2½" to 7" high.

Plate 615. The large Father Christmas in the center is marked "Printed in Germany" and is 6½" high. The three small heads on the bottom are 1¼" high. The figure in the white robe was printed in Austria and is 3¾" high.

Plate 616. Die-cuts are very colorful. The Father Christmas figures in the yellow and brown robes are unusual. The print with the children is 5" high. The smallest figure is 2" high, and the largest is 6" high.

Plate 617. Die-cuts were produced and sold in sheets. This colorful die-cut sheet contains individual Father Christmas figures which are just 1¼" high. Notice the little tabs which connect the individual figures.

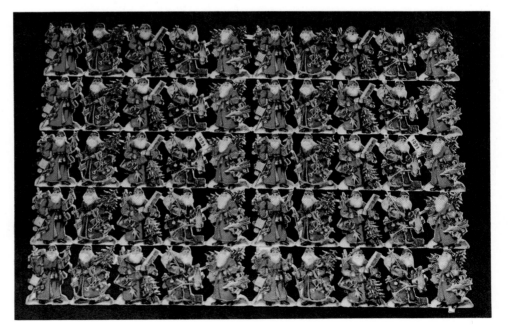

Plate 618. The tabs with the printer's indentifying marks are still connecting these large Father Christmas die-cuts. There are four different scenes on this one sheet. The figures are 9" high and were printed in Germany.

Plate 619. The Father Christmas figure in the frame is 10½" tall. The heads are still in their original sheets with their connecting tabs. Notice the printer's identifying marks are on these tabs. The heads on the left are 3½" high, and the ones on the right measure 6".

Plate 620. These two large-size German die-cuts exhibit excellent detail. Specifically, notice expecially all the colorful toys and the bee in the beard of the Santa on the left. The figure on the right has some dark hair showing from under his hood. Left, 12"; Right, 6½".

Plate 621. In some parts of the world Santa came by mule. From the looks of his burden it's probably good he has found other more modern types of transportation. This die-cut is 9½" high and 7½" wide.

Plate 622. Santa is busy examining his bag of toys. This die-cut has been nicely framed. It is 15" high and 9" wide.

Plate 623. Old scrapbooks often reveal many of the secrets of Christmas past. This die-cut of two angellic children was found mounted in an old scrapbook. The print is 12" high.

Plate 624. This page from an early scrap book shows old die-cuts. Scrapbooks were a popular place to keep die-cuts and are the reason they are sometimes referred to as "scraps." The figure in the center is 7" high, and the smaller ones are 2" high.

Plate 625. This die-cut illustrates the custom of Father Christmas bringing the presents and the tree to the children on Christmas Eve. The print is 12" high.

Plate 626. Advertising greeting cards were important give-aways for many merchants around Christmas. Elaborate decorations such as this reminded the customers to be faithful to the retailer.

Plate 627. Angels and cherubs were a favorite subject of the German printers. The figure on the left is 14" high and the one on the right is 9½" high.

Plate 628. Die-cuts which folded flat were convenient for easy storage. This nativity scene is all one-piece and is made of heavy cardboard. It is 14" tall and 22" wide.

Plate 629. This later die-cut was printed in Germany. It lacks the finer detail of some of the earlier prints and was probably made in the 1920's. It is 11" high.

Plate 630. Fold-outs such as this stand-up greeting were popular during the 1920's. This card was printed in Germany and is 16" high and 10" wide.

Plate 631. Large pressed cardboard Santa figures were often used as store displays. This example is covered with velvet. It is 21" high and was made by the Whitman Publishing Company of Racine, Wisconsin.

Plate 632. Many styles of pressed cardboard jolly-looking Santa figures were made. This figure is 14" high.

Plate 633. The pressed cardboard Santa on the left was made in Germany. It is 10" high. The scene to the right shows Santa in a sleigh being pulled by reindeer. This figure is 9" long. Both of these pieces are from the 1930's.

Plate 634. The two decorations in this photo are similar to the ones on the left. However, these are much earlier and exhibit finer detail.

Plate 635. Merchants gave their customers cards at Christmas which were suitable for hanging or framing. These two cute children are on promotional cards distributed by L. Lesquereux, 112 South High Street, Columbus, OH. They are dated December 1, 1890.

Plate 636. Santa's pouch contained a variety of entertaining greetings for the lucky child who received this card.

Plate 637. Cards with Christmas greetings are often attached to presents. These cards were designed for that purpose and date from the late 1940's to early 1950's.

225

Christmas Prints

Prints of Christmas scenes are becoming increasingly popular. Magazine covers and illustations from books and magazines are being collected and framed. These are complementing a limited supply of old commercially produced prints.

Plate 638. Print titled "Christmas Comes But Once a Year." Dated 1894, signed Pears. 18" x 36".

Plate 639. Christmas print of girl with puppies. 18" x 22".

Plate 640. "His First Christmas"

Plate 641. "Four Seasons Calendar," drawn for *St. Nicholas* magazine by Maud Humphrey.

Plate 642. Print signed Maud Humphrey and dated 1898. 8" x 10".

Plate 643. Print of little girl with large red bonnet by Maud Humphrey, copyright, 1888, by Fredrick A. Stokes & Brother. 8" x 10".

Plate 644. Maud Humphrey print of little girls inspecting a stocking. Copyright, 1890, by Fredrick Stokes & Brother. 11" x 14".

Plate 646. "My New Bonnet," print from a painting by Marie Cornelissen. 11½" x 15".

Plate 645. Christmas cover from the *London Illustrated News*, December, 1893. "A Christmas Rose." 13" x 18"

Plate 647. Unusual lithographed stove pipe cover. Diameter, 7".

Plate 648. Tapestry featuring Santa with a teddy bear and other toys. This tapestry has been reproduced recently, 9" x 19".

Prints From Children's Christmas Books

Plate 649. Family gathering around the Christmas tree, 9" x 11". Santa decorating the tree, 9" x 11".

Plate 650. Santa stuffing the stocking, 9" x 11". Santa and his reindeer arriving, 9" x 11".

Plate 651. Santa Claus reading his mail, Copyright, 1899. McLoughlin Brothers, 9" x 11". Santa Claus filling the stockings, Copyright, 1901. McLoughlin Brothers, 9" x 11".

Plate 652. Santa Claus busy in his workshop, 9" x 11". The children all snug in their beds, 9" x 11".

Plate 653. St. Nicholas climbing down the chimney, 9" x 11". Santa opening his bag of toys, 9" x 11".

Plate 654. Santa waving good-bye, 9" x 11".

Books

A vast number of children's books of Christmas stories have been published over the last century. The most collectible ones are the older books with large full-color prints. As a matter of fact, many of the more desirable books have been taken apart, and the pictures have been framed.

Two of the more popular publishers were Raphael Tuck and McLoughlin Brothers. The most commonly found book is probably *The Night Before Christmas*. This popular poem has been reprinted many times through the years.

Plate 655. *The Night Before Christmas*, printed by McLoughlin Brothers, Copyright, 1896. To the right is a print from the book.

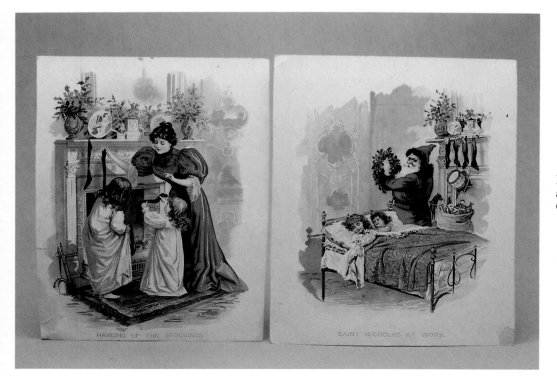

Plate 656. Prints from the above book, *The Night Before Christmas*.

Plate 657. Left: *Holly and Mistletoe*, Belford Clark and Company, Chicago. Left center: *Jolly Santa Claus*, Charles E. Graham and Co. Right center: *The Robin's Christmas Eve*, McLoughlin Brothers, New York. Right: *The Night Before Christmas*, M.A. Donahue and Co.

Plate 658. Left: *A Gift From St. Nicholas*, McLoughlin Brothers, 1899. Right: *The Night Before Christmas and Other Happy Rhymes From Childhood*, W.E. Skull, 1911.

Plate 659. Left: *Dennison's Christmas Book*, a book of Christmas ideas sold by Dennison Stores, Framingham, MA. Right: *Santa's Book*, contains "The Night Before Christmas," was a gift from Eureka Stores, Windber, PA.

Plate 660. *Christmas Time in Action* and the inside of the book.

Plate 661. Left: *Santa Claus and the Lost Kitten*, Whitman Publishing Co., 1952. Right: *Santa Claus*, Whitman Publishing Co., 1947.

Plate 662. Rear: *Santa's Tuney Toy*, Polygraphic Company of America, Inc., 1956. Front: *Santa's Circus*, White Plains Greeting Card Co., 1952.

Plate 663. *Visions of St. Nick in Action*, Philips Publishers, Inc., 1950.

Postcards

John Horsley is credited by most historians with designing the first postcard for commercial sale in 1843. This first card was a Christmas greeting postcard made for Sir Henry Cole. The card contained three separate scenes which were lithographed and then hand painted. About one thousand copies of the card were sold for one shilling each.

The use of the postcard for communication was aided by the invention of the adhesive-backed stamp in 1847, but the general acceptance of the postcard was not practical until 1899. It was during that year that Raphael Tuck convinced the British postal service to accept private-issue postcards for normal delivery. The United States Postal Service also adopted the reduced rate, and the growth in the use of decorative, privately printed postcards for use as greetings was phenomenal. The popularity of postcards peaked just before World War I,

and most of the collectible cards are from this era.

The variety of cards produced was only limited by the imagination of the manufacturers. Since many of these cards are still available in good supply today, most collectors are specializing in cards of a certain style. Some people collect cards which depict Santa Claus in a suit of a color other than red, or he may have an unusual means of transportation such as a balloon, car, or airplane. Others want artist signed cards. Two popular artists who lent their talents to postcard designs were Frances Brundage and Ellen Clapsaddle. Postcards featuring a black Santa Claus are very desirable.

One type of card which is not commonly found reveals a hidden picture when the card is held up to a strong light. These are usually expensive if they are found in good shape.

Plate 664. The two cards on the bottom are copyrighted by John Winsch. One is dated 1910, and the other is from 1913.

Plate 665. The two cards on the top are artist signed. The card on the left is by Frances Brundage, and the one on the right was designed by Ellen Clapsaddle.

Plate 666. Father Christmas in various color suits. Top left: Printed in Germany. Series 1480. Circa 1910. Top right: Printed in Germany. Series 1826. Circa 1912. Bottom left: Printed in Germany. Nn 4774. Circa 1909. Bottom: Printed in Germany. P.S. Dresden Series No. 4896.

Plate 667. Top left: Santa in unusual white suit. Series 213-A. Top right: Santa. Circa 1912. Bottom left: Series 213. Dated 1912. Bottom right: Series 61-D. This Santa sports a pipe.

Plate 668. Top left: Printed in Germany, 1915. Top right: Printed in Germany. Christmas seal dated 1915. Bottom left: Made in U.S.A., Dated 1916. Bottom right: Dated 1909. Shows an early Santa with a long robe.

Plate 669. Top left: No. 6607, Circa 1912. Top right: Circa 1912. Bottom left: Santa arriving in a modified hot air balloon. Bottom right: Santa in a long green robe. About 1910.

Plate 670. Bottom left: "Nimble Nicks." 1920's Whitney Made, Worcester, MA. Bottom right: A very desirable "LOOK THRO" type card. Printed in Germany.

Plate 671. Colorful old cards like these are sought after by many collectors. They are inexpensive additions which are a complement to any collection.

Plate 672. These cards picture Santa arriving by auto and sleigh. The card in the top left illustrates a hard to find black Santa Claus. All these cards are dated prior to WWI.

238

Plate 673. Top left: Printed in Germany. 1911. Top right: Made in Germany. Bottom left: Series 227-F, 1911. Bottom right: A & S, 1908. Notice the very fancy red robe.

Plate 674. Top right: Printed in Germany. Tanner Souvenir Co., New York. Bottom left: Raphael Tuck & Sons, Christmas Postcard Series No. 136. Printed in Saxony.

239

Plate 675. Top left: Printed in Germany. Top right: Printed in Germany. Bottom right: Int. Art Publishing Co., New York-Philadelphia.

Plate 676. The card on the bottom left is unusual since it features a black Santa Claus.

Plate 677. Top left: Printed in Saxony. No. 729. Top right: Copyright, 1910 by Arthur Horwitz. Bottom left: Printed in Saxony. Bottom right: Printed in Germany.

Plate 678. Notice the embossed poodle representing the gift-giver in the top left. The bottom right postcard features a Father Christmas in a nicely decorated long brown robe.

241

Plate 679. These cards are from the Christmas Delight series of 1907.

Plate 680. This is a series of bronze and silver cards featuring Santa in a wreath bearing joyful proclamations of the season.

242

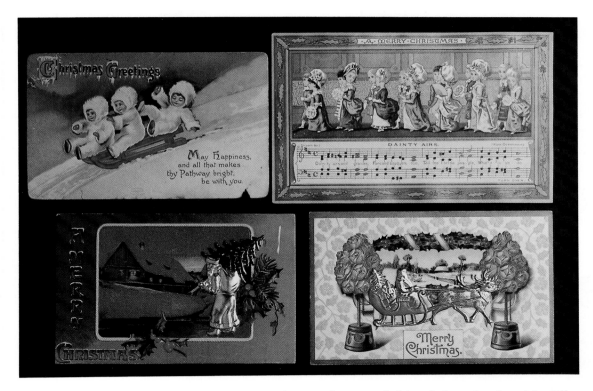

Plate 681. The card on the top left features the popular snow babies. It is artist signed by Ellen Clapsaddle. The card on the bottom left pictures the German custom with Father Christmas bringing the tree on Christmas Eve.

Plate 682. Some cards were meant to be humorous as is demonstrated by these cards from the mid-twenties.

Trade Cards

Postcard-like cards were often given away by merchants during the holidays as a gesture of goodwill and to promote their businesses. These cards were usually slightly larger then postcards and were not meant to be sent through the mail. These cards are called trade cards. They are collectible, and since most of the trade cards were not produced in very large quantities, most of them are much harder to find than regular postcards.

Cards from large manufacturers and individual merchants will be found. Usually the hardest cards to find will be those of the small retailer who only had a few hundred customers to whom to give his cards. Many times cards of this type will only have local appeal, but they may command very high prices in their specific region. Cards from large manufacturers usually have a larger market. However, they are more common. Therefore, the price collectors will pay for these is usually lower.

Plate 683. These two trade cards are from the Woolson Spice Company of Toledo, OH, manufacturer of Lion Coffee. The card on the left is copyrighted 1890, by Kapp & Co., NY. The Christmas trade card on the right is from 1891. It was produced by Donaldson Brothers of New York.

Plate 684. This picture shows the reverse side of the above two trade cards featuring the Woolson Spice company's pitch for Lion Coffee.

Plate 685. These three trade cards are from the late 1800's and early 1900's. They were given free each year to anyone who bought a one pound package of Lion Coffee. The cards are about 5" wide by 7" long. The oldest and best quality of these cards is the one on the left. This card was released during the Christmas season in 1888.

Plate 686. This picture shows the reverse side of the cards above and below. Notice the center card with the "Certificate of Purity" for Lion Coffee.

Plate 687. These cards are Woolson Spice Company advertising trade cards from the early 1900's. They are a little smaller than the earlier cards at 4½" by 7", and the detail is not quite as sharp.

Plate 688. These trade cards were given out by Schultz & Co. of Zanesville, OH, producers of Star soap. They are from the early 1900's and measure 5" by 7".

Plate 689. The trade card on the left was given away by a local merchant – M.E. de Vyver – of Mount Vernon, OH. A free chance on a piano was being offered to all customers who made a minimum purchase of one dollar. The card also promoted the store's line of Christmas merchandise. The trade card in the center hawked the coffee and spices of the C.F. Ware Coffee Co. of Dayton, OH. The card on the right sported a sure cure of all types of ailments. John F. Patton, Medicine Maker, York, PA was the proud promotor.

Plate 690. This photo illustrates the reverse side of the above cards. Pay special attention to the one on the right if you are a hypochondriac.

Advertising
The Coca-Cola Influence

By the beginning of the 1920's the tremendous commercial appeal and excellent salesmanship of jolly old St. Nick was starting to be utilized by several large corporations. Coca-Cola was perhaps the leader in recognizing the full potential of the mass appeal of Santa Claus. Their Christmas ads, which have appeared each year since the early 1930's, have helped to shape and mold the image of this annual nocturnal visitor in the minds of all Americans. Of course, we have learned over the last fifty years that Christmas is just not complete without Santa and a "Coke."

The following photographs are from the back cover of the December issues of the *National Geographic* magazine. The series pictured features Coca-Cola ads from 1933 to 1964.

Plate 691. 1933 – AWAY with a TIRED THIRSTY FACE; 1934 – The pause that keeps you going – with tingling bouyancy; 1935 – It will refresh you, too; 1936 – Old Santa says, "Me too."

Plate 692. 1937 – "Give and take," say I; 1938. Thanks for the pause that refreshes; 1939 – And the same to you; 1940 – Somebody knew I was coming.

Plate 693. 1941 – Thirst asks nothing more; 1942 – That Extra Something; 1944 – Have a "Coke" = Merry Christmas; 1945 – Christmas together... Have a Coca-Cola.

Plate 694. 1947 – Hospitality in your refrigerator; 1948 – Where there's Coca-Cola there's hospitality; 1949 – Travel refreshed; 1950 – For Santa.

Plate 695. 1951 – ... talk about being good!; 1952 – ... and now the gift for thirst; 1953 – The pause that refreshes; 1954 – It's my gift for thirst.

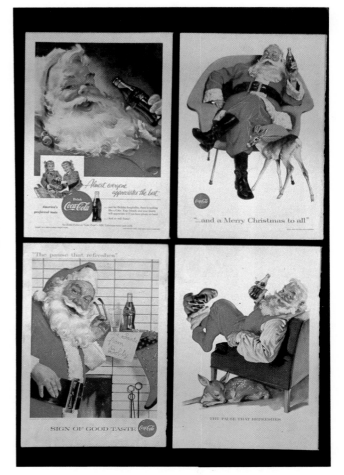

Plate 696. 1955 – Almost everyone appreciates the best; 1956 – ...and a Merry Christmas to all; 1957 – SIGN OF GOOD TASTE; 1958 – THE PAUSE THAT REFRESHES.

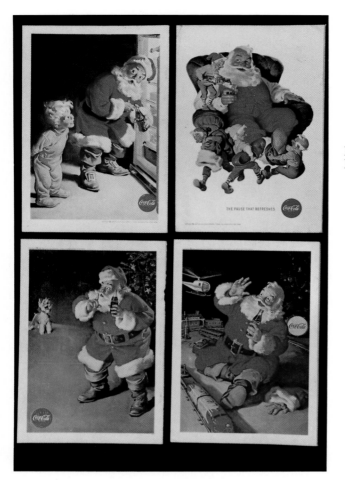

Plate 697. 1959 – untitled; 1960 – THE PAUSE THAT REFRESHES; 1961 – untitled; 1962 – untitled.

Plate 698. 1963 – things go better with Coke; 1964 – things go better with Coke.

Whitman Candies also incorporated Santa Claus in their advertising. The change in appearance of their Santa over the period of seventeen years is obvious. His extra weight may be the result of too many of their sweets.

Plate 699. Whitman's Candy ad, Copyright, 1917, S.F. Whitman & Son, Inc.

Plate 700. Whitman's Candy ad from 1934.

Plate 701. General Electric promotion for Christmas lights in 1938.

Plate 702. Santa Claus even came to town on the tip of a General Electric Christmas bulb in 1949.

Plate 703. Noma advertising promoting Christmas decorations was colorful and enthusiastic as demonstrated by this ad.

Plate 704. Interwoven Corporation was a great believer in the powers of Santa Claus. Even the trials of WWII could not dampen his spirit.

252

Christmas Seals

Christmas seals are the adhesive-backed decorative stamps which are sent out by the American Lung Association in their annual fund raising campaign. The idea of using stamps for this purpose was developed in 1903 by Elina Holboell, a Danish postmaster. The first seals were printed the next year and sold in his native Denmark.

Seals were introduced to the American public in 1907 by Emily Bissel and philanthropist Jacob Riis for the benefit of the American Red Cross. By 1919 the sole benefactor of the stamps was the National Tuberculosis Association, forerunner of the present day American Lung Association. The Cross of Lorraine – symbol of Godfrey Lorraine, a leader in the First Crusade – was chosen for their emblem.

Shown in the photographs below are an advertisement for Christmas seals from 1920. This was sponsored by the Tuberculosis Association which had just adopted this version of the Lorraine cross as its symbol. Notice a seal from 1915 shown on a postcard on page 237 bears the Red Cross emblem. The picture on the right shows examples of Christmas seals from the years 1935, 1937, 1938, and 1943.

Plate 705. Advertisement for Christmas Seals from 1920.

Plate 706. Examples of Christmas Seals from 1935, 1937, 1938, and 1943.

China – Glass – Metal
Decorative Lamps

Plate 707. These Santa lamps were popular decorative items during the 1920's and 1930's. The lamp on the left is all-glass and is 8" high. The lamp in the center was made by the U.S. Glass company from about 1923 until the 1930's. It is 10½" high. The lamp on the right is a figural bulb with a celluloid base. It was made in Japan and was available in a variety of colors. The original box is marked "Tree Lighting Lamp, Edison Base Santa Claus." This lamp is 9½" high.

As America became electrified, lamps began to replace candles in many homes. Some of the lamps produced during the late 1920's and early 1930's were very elaborate. There were glass shades and bulbs made in the shape of Santa. Since many of the bulbs were discarded when they burned out and the shades cracked if too strong a bulb was used, these figural lamps are not often found today.

America was becoming very aware of the danger of fire from candles in the 1920's. Clusters of candle-like lamps and wreaths with small lights representing candles were used in place of real candles. These were produced in great abundance and are found quite frequently today.

Plate 708. The wreathe on the left is made of cast iron. It is 8¾" high. The lamp on the right is a Christmas tree with a moon and star decoration. Notice the Santa figures on the corners of the cast iron base. The lamp is 11" high.

Plate 709. This heavy cast iron wreath could either be hung on the wall or set in the window.

Plate 710. This triangular-shaped lighting device was wrapped with plastic pine needles to produce a holiday look.

Plate 711. This coated cardboard lamp is 11" high and was made in Japan.

Plate 712. Special holiday bulbs were made for regular lamps.

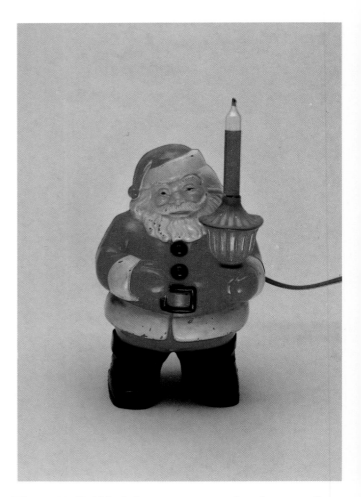

Plate 714. Bubble lights were so popular that even Santa had to have one. This plastic lamp from the 1950's is 8" high.

Plate 713. These Paramount outdoor candles have a Bakelite base and are 42" high.

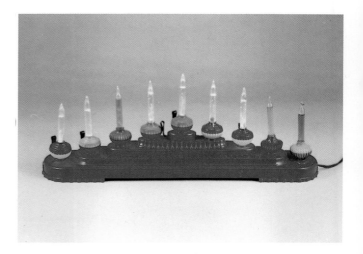

Plate 715. Bubble lights were sold in just about every conceivable manner. These were designed to be placed in a window or on a mantle.

Plate 716. This plastic decoration has Santa holding a tree between two candles.

Plate 717. Noma produced this decoration. A plastic Santa which lights is standing between two bottle brush trees.

Plate 718. Rudolph has a very bright nose. This is expecially true for this night light produced by E.M.C. Art. Length, 12" high.

Plate 719. Wreaths made of chenille were common decorations after World War II. These decorations can still be found for reasonable prices.

Plate 720. NOMA had a light for every occasion. Anyone lucky enough to own a car could surely afford to decorate it.

258

Plate 721. Battery operated signal lanterns were made in a variety of styles. Most of these were made in Japan. The lamp on the right uses Christmas lights with a C-6 base. These lamps were made after World War II.

Plate 722. Santa figural signal lamps are beginning to be collectible. These were made in the late 1940's and early 1950's.

Plate 723. The plastic and tin lamp on the left was made during the 1950's by the Glo-Light Corporation of Chicago. It is 8½" high. The lamp on the right is made of plastic and is 6" high.

259

Children's Dishes, Pottery, and Glass

Collectors are continously expanding their interests, and many of them are now searching for all kinds of Christmas related items to add to their collections. Many collectors have been turning to the numerous types of china and glass items that have been made for the holidays. An added attraction is that many of these items are functional as well as decorative.

The quality and beauty of German children's tea sets has been appreciated by collectors of children's dishes for years. Lately, these small tea sets with Christmas decals have been attracting the attention of Christmas collectors. Although their appeal is high, so are their prices. The most desirable tea sets were made around the turn century, and their current availability is almost non-existent.

Cookie jars, teapots, bowls, stirrers, cups and other items featuring Christmas scenes are also being collected. Some pieces are not very old, but if the piece is attractive and the price is not excessive, age makes very little difference to some people.

Plate 724. Santa's favorite forms of transportation are pictured. This pink luster child's tea set was made in Germany during the early 1900's.

Plate 725. Some German children's tea sets were very fancy. The decal is Mary and Joseph, and the pieces bear the greeting "Merry Christmas."

Plate 726. Various shades of the same decal are sometimes found on early tea sets. This children's "Merry Christmas" set was made in Germany in the early 1900's.

Plate 727. This set has the same decal as the set in the previous photo. However, the shape of the pieces and their size is different. The same decal was often used on different blanks, sometimes by different manufacturers.

Plate 728. Three different scenes – children with a snowman, two children on sleds, and Santa pulling a sled – are depicted on this early German child's set.

Plate 729. The backstamp on these pieces of a child's tea set is "Leuchtenberg, Germany." The set bears the greeting "Merry Christmas" and is finished with green luster.

Plate 730. Pink luster sets with Christmas greetings are very desirable. This set is from the same blank as the one to the left. It is from the early 1900's.

Plate 731. Holly-decorated children's pieces make an interesting Christmas display. This set was made in Germany in the early 1900's.

Plate 732. Cups and saucers of various shapes bearing a Christmas greeting are being collected. These are from various German children's tea sets.

Plate 733. Lone cups and saucers reveal there are still more German children's Christmas tea sets waiting to be found by some lucky collector.

Plate 734. American potteries also produced sets with Christmas decals. These cups and saucers are part of a miniature set which was probably made in the late 1940's or early 1950's by Universal Pottery of Cambridge, OH.

Plate 735. Roseville Pottery of Zanesville, OH produced numerous sets of juvenile dishes from 1916 until the mid 1930's. Their Christmas set featured a decal of Santa Claus.

Plate 736. The rear side of these two holly decorated-pieces is marked "Watt Pottery Company, Christmas 1957."

Plate 737. The Hall China Company of East Liverpool, OH made kitchenware accessories with a holly design during the 1950's.

Plate 738. This dinnerware set was made by the Hall China Company of East Leverpool, OH during the 1950's.

Plate 739. Taylor, Smith and Taylor produced this "Holly and Spruce" party set during the mid 1960's. The 12 piece set we have in the original box included 4 cups and saucers and 4 - 8" plates. Notice the cups and saucers only have the holly design while the plates have a decal which features a Christmas tree with presents under it.

Plate 740. Southern Potteries of Erwin, TN produced several hand painted Christmas dinnerware sets during the 1950's and 1960's. These Christmas sets are very collectible today.

Plate 741. This Santa beverage set includes a pitcher and four mugs. The set is unmarked, but the facial expression of the Santa and quality of the pottery seem to indicate it was made by the American Bisque Company.

Plate 742. Santa heads make attractive cookie jars, and American potteries developed various styles. The Santa on the right was produced by the American Bisque Company, and the maker of the other one is unknown.

Plate 743. The backstamp on this teapot reads "Lucky Santa Claus Teapot," Made in England, Reg. No. 835362." It is 7" high.

Plate 744. Pictured in this photo is an early English cream pitcher. The container is a large bag on Santa's back, and the pour spout is at the top of his head. 8" high.

Plate 745. China and pottery heads are becoming increasingly collectible. These heads were made in Japan during the 1950's and 1960's.

Plate 746. Colorful china heads are attractive Christmas decorations. These three heads exhibit quality and fine detail.

Plate 747. These delightful gift-laden girls were imported from Japan by Napco distributing of Cleveland, OH.

Plate 748. American glass companies produced numerous items for children. The tumblers were made by Hazel Atlas from their "Hoppy" tumbler blank. The bowl was made by Corning Glass at their Charleroi, PA plant.

Plate 749. Glass stirrers have been made for many years, and some similar to the Santa heads are still being made. However, most of the newer ones lack the detail of the older ones.

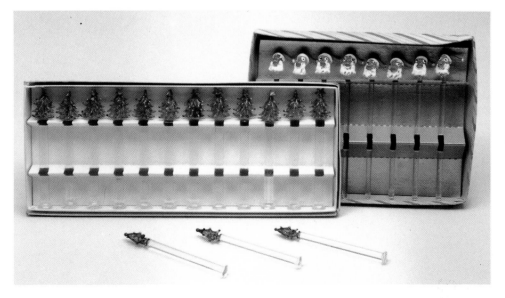

Danish Christmas Silverware

In 1910, a series of silver spoons and forks was intiated by the Michelson Silver Company of Denmark, a well known silver company at the turn of the century. Michelson Silver was already the official "Jeweler of the Royal Danish Court" and had been entrusted with making all the official Danish state decorations since 1846.

The first series, "the Star of Bethlehem," was not dated, since the idea of a yearly issues was not planned when the Christmas design was conceived. However, the first issue was so successful that yearly spoons and forks have been produced. Each year an outstanding Danish craftsman has been chosen to produce a unique design for the company.

Each spoon and fork is made of sterling silver imported from Mexico. Notice many of the spoons feature elaborate art work, and some are richly enhanced with beautiful enamel. Each piece is 6" long and weighs 1½" ounces.

Before 1975, when the company started making spoons and forks for the current year only, items from previous years could be ordered.

Plate 750. Left to right: 1. 1910 spoon, "The Star of Bethelhem," designed by N.C. Dyrlund. 2. 1912 spoon, "Christmas Bells," designed by Paul Michelson. 3. 1912 fork, "Christmas Bells," designed by Paul Michelson. 4. 1913 spoon, "Christmas Scenery," designed by Paul Michelson.

Plate 751. Left to right: 1. 1915 spoon, "The Three Kings of Cologne," designed by H. Slott-Moller. 2. 1916 fork, "The Madonna," designed by Marie Henriques. 3. 1916 spoon, "The Madonna," designed by Marie Henriques. 4. 1925 spoon, "Poinsetta," designed by Ellen Michelson.

Plate 752. Left to right: 1. 1929 spoon, "Christmas Rose," designed by Ebba Holm. 2. 1933 spoon, "The Little Match Girl," designed by Ib Lunding. 3. 1933 fork, "The Little Match Girl," designed by Ib Lunding. 4. 1939 spoon, "The Gift-Laden Christmas Tree," designed by O-Staehr-Nielson.

Plate 753. Left to right: 1. 1954 spoon, "Cornets," designed by Loren Lass. 2. 1959 spoon, "The Lucia Bride," designed by Henry Thelander. 3. 1965 spoon. 4. 1966 spoon. 5. 1967 spoon. 6. 1968 spoon.

Costume Jewelry

Inexpensive costume jewelry became the rage in the 1930's when consumers were bearing the hardships of the Great Depression. Women still wanted attractive jewelry, but only the wealthy could afford gold. Colorful costume jewelry was designed to fit every occasion, and Christmas was no exception. Popular subjects included Santa, snowmen, reindeer, angels, bells, wreaths, Christmas trees, candles, boots, and holly. Many of the pieces were also decorated with sparkling rhinestones. Today many collectors wear examples from their collection over the holiday period.

Plate 754. Unusual Santa figures, such as the Black Santa, or one with a popular manufacturer's name are especially desirable.

Plate 755. Many different styles of Santa heads were made.

Plate 756. Many of these angel pins are accented with rhinestones.

Plate 757. Reindeer heads were often trimmed with holly or embedded with rhinestones.

Plate 758. Full-figure reindeer are attractive pins.

271

Plate 759. Many pins were made in the shape of bells.

Plate 760. This picture shows various examples of holly pins.

Plate 761. Boots were often filled with articles of the holiday season.

Plate 762. Holiday candles were often combined with holly to produce attractive pins.

Plate 763. Holiday wreaths in the form of pins are very colorful.

Plate 764. Rhinestones were often combined in an interesting manner to produce pins in the form of snowflakes, candles, trees, and wreaths.

Cake and Candy Molds

Cakes, cookies and chocolate candy always have been popular gifts for children. Therefore, many molds have been designed through the years to produce the variety of Christmas figures children love. Santa molds are found most commonly. Other molds, which may be found, include reindeer, Christmas trees, and angels. Molds were usually made from cast iron, tin, or pewter. However, some of the later molds were made of aluminum. Many people are now collecting these old molds and hanging them on their walls for decoration.

Plate 765. These tin chocolate molds are probably from the 1920's or early 1930's. The teddy bear mold is a two-piece mold and is 5½" high. The other two molds of Santa with a basket are double hinged. The large one is 9" high, and the small one is 8" high.

Plate 767. This Santa mold is made of aluminum and is 11½" high. It is marked "Santa Claus Cake Mold" and was made by Nordic-Ware, Minneapolis, MN.

Plate 766. The small mold on the left is a 3" high tin Santa mold. The mold in the center is made of cast iron and is 12" high. It was made by the Griswold manufacturing Company, Erie, PA. The mold on the right is 4½" high. It is a Santa mold and is made of cast iron.

Plate 768. Christmas trees, reindeer, and Santa Claus were popular designs for holiday baked goods. The large cake tins are 9" in diameter, and the small one is 3". The tree-shaped pan on the right is marked "Mirro-Finest Aluminum."

Miscellaneous

Plate 769. Father Christmas is busy entertaining the children in the scene from this old cardboard utility box. The box is 6" square.

Plate 770. Well-preserved advertising boxes from the late 1800's are not easy to find. This large box is 16" square and 12" deep.

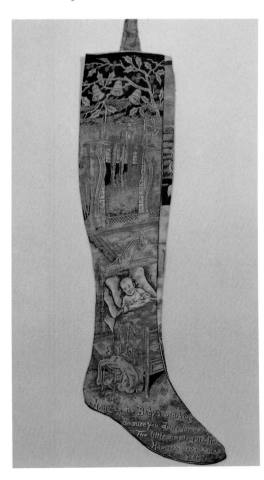

Plates 771 & 772. There are different scenes on each side of this cotton stocking. It is 24" long, so there should be plenty of space for all of St. Nick's goodies.

Plate 773. Some Santa figures were cast from plaster molds such as this one. 6" high.

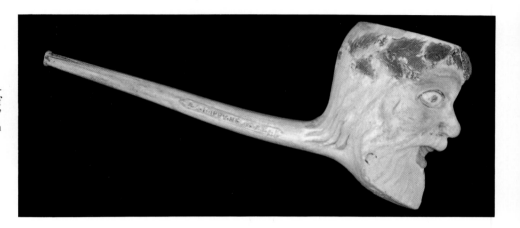

Plate 774. This unusual, holly-decorated Father Christmas pipe is made of clay. It is marked "Merry Christmas" on one side and "Happy New Year" on the other. 11" long.

Plate 775. Tinsel-decorated composition dolls were often set in the branches of trees. Little girls could also play with these dolls. 11" high.

Plate 776. Miniature working record players allowed children to play their favorite Christmas music. This Bing model is 6½" square.

Glossary

Belsnickle (Pelsnickle) is the modern pronunciation of Pelze Nicol.

Bisque is a pottery term referring to clay which has been fired, but is unglazed. The result is a matte finish.

Cellophane is a treated cellulose material that has been pressed into thin transparent strips. These were used for the production of artificial Christmas trees and other decorative ornaments.

Celluloid is a name for a hard, semi-elastic, plastic-like material which was used primarily for small figural decorations.

Chenille is a soft fuzzy, velvety cord used for decorations. Support for chenille figures is usually achieved by wrapping this cord around a thin wire.

Chromo is a collector term referring to colorful chromolithographed paper decorations which were a product of the printing revolution, which began in the last half of the nineteenth century.

Composition dolls have a foundation of papier-mache, which has been covered with a thin layer of liquid plaster to produce a smooth finish.

Die-Cut is another term for "chromo." Since they were stamped out by a die during the printing process, these flat paper decorations are often called "die-cuts."

Dresden is a term collectors use to identify paper ornaments made with a shiny metallic type of paper.

Father Christmas became one of the new names for the gift-giver during the Christmas season following the Protestant Reformation.

Feather Tree is a type of artificial tree usually made from dyed goose or turkey feathers.

Festoon is a pre-wired string of Christmas tree lights.

Kalends was the Roman celebration of the New Year. It began on January first and lasted three days.

Kriss Kringle is an English pronunciation for "Christkindchen" – the German Christ Child, who was the gift-giver in parts of Germany and among the Pennslyvania Dutch.

Kugel is a heavy silvered glass ornament made in Germany during the last half of the nineteenth century. Most kugels are round, but other shapes of early heavy ornaments, such as ovals and grape clusters, are also called kugels.

Mica is a thin transparent mineral substance which was often used to add luster and enhance the reflective properties of an ornament.

Miracle Plays (mystery play) were fourteenth century plays performed outside the churches to educate the converts in the stories of the Bible.

Mithraism was one of the major religions of the Roman Empire. Mithra became god of the sun, which was worshipped in his name.

Molded cardboard decorations result from liquid paper, which is poured into molds, pressed into shape, and allowed to dry.

NOMA stands for the National Outfit Manufacturers Association, which was formed by the combination of 15 independent companies.

Papier-mache is a molded combination of pulp and glue along with other fillers. Figures are molded in two halves and joined after drying. The seams are sanded and sealed with varnish, and the finished product is painted.

Pelze Nicol is a grotesque characterization of St. Nicholas as represented in the German Christmas celebration after the Reformation. He accompanied the Christ Child and was responsible for punishing bad children.

Pere Noel became the name of the French gift-bearer after the Reformation.

Putz is a German term for the stable scene constructed under the Christmas tree. This usually consists of buildings, animals, and human figures.

Pyramids were early German decorations made from cut evergreen boughs and formed in the shape of a pyramid. These were often decorated with candles and pastries.

Reformation was the sixteenth century religious movement, which aimed at changing Catholicism and ended in the establishment of Protestantism.

Saturnalia was an annual Roman celebration which was held in December in honor of the god Saturn.

Scraps are terms given to flat chromolithographed paper decorations. These were often kept in scrapbooks and are also known as die-cuts and chromos.

Spun Glass consists of thin glass fibers often combined with scraps to form ornaments.

St. Nicholas was a bishop of Myra during the fourth century A.D. He became the first gift-giving personality associated with the holiday season.

Bibliography

Barnett, James H. *The American Christmas*. Macmillan: New York, 1954.

Brenner, Robert. *Christmas Past*. Schiffer Publishing Ltd.: West Chester, Pennsylvania, 1985.

Brenner, Robert. *Christmas Revisited*. Schiffer Publishing, Ltd: West Chester, Pennsylvania, 1986.

Court, Earl W. *4000 Years of Christmas*. Schuman: New York, 1948.

Del Re, Patricia and Gerard. *The Christmas Almanack*. Doubleday and Company, Inc.: Garden City, New York, 1979.

Hole, Christina. *Christmas and Its Customs*. M. Barrows and Company, Inc.: New York, 1958.

Hottes, Alfred Carl. *One Thousand and One Christmas Facts and Fancies*. Dodd, Mead & Company: New York, 1944.

Ickis, Marguerite. *The Book of Festival Holidays*. Dodd, Mead & Company: New York, 1964.

Johnson, George. *Christmas Ornaments, Lights, & Decorations*. Collector Books: Paducah, Kentucky, 1987.

Joseph, Robert. *The Christmas Book*. McAfee Books: New York, 1978.

Lewis, Floyd A. *The Incandescent Light*. Shorewood: New York, 1949.

Meyers, Robert J. *Celebrations: The Complete Book of American Holidays*. Doubleday & Company, Inc.: Garden City, New York, 1972.

Miles, Clement A. *Christmas Customs and Tradition: Their History and Significance*. Dover Publications: New York, 1976.

Rogers, Maggie, with Judith Hawkins. *The Glass Christmas Ornament: Old and New*. Timber Press: Forest Grove, Oregon, 1979.

Snyder, Phillip V. *The Christmas Tree Book*. The Viking Press: New York, 1976.

Winkler, John. *Five and Ten: The Fabulous Life of F.W. Woolworth*. McBride: New York, 1940.

Index

Price Guide

Points to Remember

Condition of the decoration and an individual's desire to own the item are the two most important influences in determining prices.

Prices indicated in this guide are for articles in generally good condition – not necessarily the condition in which they are pictured. Many of the early and more desirable decorations are now around a hundred years old, and they have been used and abused for many years. Most are made of paper or glass and are extremely fragile. Sometimes condition is difficult to evaluate, but if there are parts missing, or if the item is broken or repaired, then it should obviously be worth less than the price listed in this guide.

Considerably harder to evaluate are the whims and fancies of collectors who buy these collectibles. In almost every collectible field, there are three basic groups of collectors. There are a few individuals who will pay any amount of money to amass a very large collection. They pay huge sums for choice items, and word of these fantastic prices spreads like wildfire throughout the market. At the other extreme, there are some who prefer to spend very little on their collections. They continuously seek bargains and are thrilled by the "sleepers" they find. Sandwiched between these two extremes are the majority of the collectors. These individuals prefer to pay reasonable prices for most of their collection. They have worked hard for years to accumulate their treasures. A few pieces have been found at a bargain and a few others at a premium.

Advertisements have been checked. Auction results have been noted. Collectors and dealers have been consulted, and various tales have been heard. The intention has been to produce a price guide which is equitable. However, you as the collector or dealer are the final judge as to the value of an item.

St. Nicholas – Father Christmas – Kriss Kringle – Santa Claus

Some of the early German Father Christmas figures are among the highest priced Christmas collectibles. Especially desirable are the turn-of-the-century clock-works nodders and the papier-mache belsnickles. Belsnickles vary widely in price. Much of this variation is determined by size, color, and quality of molding. The belsnickles which are bringing the highest prices are those in unusual colors or with exceptionally sharply moded details. Commonly found colors are red, blue, gray, gold, and white. Unusual colors are black, green, pink, and lavender.

Other highly desirable items include items such as banks, dolls, and toys. These fall into a "double collectible" category. As a result, there is an increased demand for these items, and the prices are inflated. Some of the more popular and more moderately priced items are those pieces which were made in the United States and Japan during the twenties and thirties. Also, in recent years Santa collectibles from the 1950's and 1960's have begun to attract collector interest.

The date of manufacture is indicated in the price guide below. These approximate dates are included to help collectors determine the time period when these figures were produced. It should be remembered that some pieces may have been made for long periods of time, and these dates should not be interpreted as the exact and only years of manufacture.

Although there are some new "old-type" Father Christmas figures on the market, they are not presenting much of a problem for collectors. Most of these new pieces are doll-like figures made by private individuals. Even though many are made to look old, a quick examination of their clothing and compostion is all that is necessary to determine their recent vintage.

Plate No.		Date	Country	Size	Price
1.	Left	late 1800's	Germany	12"	600.00-700.00
	Right	late 1800's	Germany	11"	700.00-750.00
2.	Left	early 1900's	Germany	8½"	400.00-500.00
	Right	early 1900's	Germany	8½"	400.00-500.00
3.	Left	late 1800's	Germany	10"	600.00-700.00
	Right	late 1800's	Germany	8"	450.00-500.00
4.	Left	circa 1900	Germany	9½"	350.00-400.00
	Center	circa 1900	Germany	8½"	500.00-600.00
	Right	circa 1900	Germany	8"	400.00-450.00
5.	Left	1890-1910	Germany	6"	275.00-325.00
	Right	circa 1900	Germany	7"	275.00-325.00
6.		1920's	Germany	9"	275.00-325.00
7.		circa 1920's	Germany	9"	300.00-400.00
8.	Left	circa 1900	Germany	6"	175.00-225.00
	Left center	early 1900's	America	9"	300.00-400.00
	Right center	1930's	Japan	6"	65.00-75.00
	Right	early 1900's	Germany	9"	275.00-325.00
9.		late 1800's	Germany	11"	1000.00-1200.00
10.		circa 1880's	Germany	7½"	400.00-450.00

Plate No.		Date	Country	Size	Price
11.	Left	circa 1900	Germany	11"	1200.00-1500.00
	Right	circa 1900	Germany	10"	1000.00-1200.00
12.		late 1800's	Germany	14½"	1400.00-1600.00
13.		early 1900's	Germany	30"	1800.00-2000.00
14.		early 1900's	Germany		1600.00-1800.00
15.		early 1900's	Germany	22"	1600.00-1800.00
16.		circa 1910	Germany	10"	400.00-600.00
17.	Left	circa 1900	Germany	29"	1800.00-2000.00
	Right	late 1800's	Germany	40"	1900.00-2200.00
18.		circa 1900	Germany	26"	1700.00-1900.00
19.		late 1800's	Germany	28"	1700.00-1900.00
20.		circa 1900	Germany	16"	1000.00-1200.00
21.	Left	circa 1900	Germany	10"	60.00-85.00
	Right	circa 1900	Germany	6½"	125.00-150.00
22.		early 1920's	Germany	8"	250.00-300.00
23.		1920's	Germany	6"	150.00-200.00
24.		late 1800's	Germany	18"	175.00-225.00
25.	Left	1920-1930's	America	21"	200.00-250.00
	Right	1930's	America	16"	300.00-350.00
26.		1930's	America	19"	300.00-350.00
27.		1940's	America		200.00-250.00
28.		1940's		31"	150.00-200.00
29.		1920's	Germany	28"	500.00-600.00
30.	Left	1920-1930's	Japan	14"	250.00-300.00
	Right	1900-1920's	Germany	10"	200.00-250.00
31.		1930's	Japan	9"	140.00-160.00
32.	Left	1930's	Japan	7"	110.00-130.00
	Center	1930's	Japan	10"	75.00-85.00
	Right	1930's	Japan	7½"	60.00-70.00
33.	Left	1930-1940's	Japan	6"	55.00-75.00
	Center	1920-1930's	Japan	7½"	110.00-130.00
	Right	1920's	Germany	5½"	65.00-85.00
34.	Left	1930's	Occ. Japan	3¾"	30.00-40.00
	Center	1930's	Japan	6½"	50.00-60.00
	Right	circa 1920	Japan	5"	50.00-75.00
35.		early 1920's	Japan	2½"	35.00-45.00
36.	Left	1930's	Japan	9" long	20.00-25.00
	Center	1930's	Germany	4"	100.00-125.00
	Right	1930's	Germany	2½"	50.00-60.00
37.		1930's	Japan	11" long	100.00-125.00
38.	Left	1930's	Japan	2¾"	45.00-55.00
	Center	1930's	Japan	3"	40.00-45.00
	Right	circa 1920	Germany	5"	100.00-125.00
39.	Left	late 1940's	W. Germany	9"	95.00-110.00
	Right	circa 1930's	Japan	6"	50.00-60.00
40.	Left	1950's	Occ. Japan	5¼"	40.00-45.00
	Center	1950's	Japan	9"	75.00-85.00
	Right	1950's	Occ. Japan	6"	60.00-70.00
41.	Left	1950's	Japan	3¼"	15.00-20.00
	Left center	1950's	Japan	4"	18.00-20.00
	Right center	1950's	Japan	6"	40.00-45.00
	Right	1930's	Japan	3½"	25.00-30.00
42.	Left	1930's	Japan	5½"	30.00-35.00
	Right	1950's	Japan	7½"	70.00-80.00
43.		1930's	Japan	9"	50.00-60.00
44.		early 1900's	Germany	12½"	200.00-250.00
45.		1940-1950's	America	10"	45.00-50.00
46.		1950's	America	18"	75.00-85.00
47.		1950-1960's		11"	35.00-40.00
48.		1930's		18"	75.00-100.00
49.		1940's	America	20"	75.00-125.00
50.		1940's	America	26"	250.00-350.00
51.		1940-1950's	America	28"	200.00-300.00
52.		early 1900's	America	16" long	250.00-300.00
	Reproduction	1920's	America	16" long	150.00-200.00

Plate No.	Date	Country	Size	Price
53.	late 1800's	America	6"	200.00-225.00
Reproduction	1930's	America	6"	100.00-125.00
54.	early 1900's	America	6"	200.00-225.00
55. Santa	1930's		2¼"	35.00-40.00
Reindeer	1930's	Germany	2½"	25.00-30.00
56.	1920-1930's	America	5½"	90.00-110.00
57.	1950's		7½"	80.00-90.00
58.			6½"	100.00-125.00
59. Left			5"	70.00-80.00
Right				85.00-95.00
60.	1950's	Japan	12"	100.00-125.00
61. Left		Japan	11½"	95.00-125.00
Right		Japan	9"	65.00-85.00
62. Left	1950's	Japan	13"	75.00-90.00
Center	1950's	Japan	10"	45.00-55.00
Right	1950's	Japan	5½"	40.00-50.00
63. Top left	1950's	Occ. Japan	4½" long	50.00-65.00
Top right	1950's	Occ. Japan	5" long	50.00-65.00
Bottom	1950's	Japan	7½"	70.00-80.00
64. Left	1950's	America	4"	35.00-45.00
Center	1950's	America	5"	35.00-45.00
Right	1950's	America	4"	28.00-37.00
65. Left		Japan	3½"	45.00-55.00
Center		Japan	4¾"	50.00-60.00
Right		Japan	7½"	80.00-95.00
66. Left		Japan	4¼"	55.00-65.00
Center		Japan	5"	100.00-150.00
Right		Japan	6¼"	80.00-100.00
67. Left			5"	70.00-80.00
Center			5"	60.00-70.00
Right			5¼"	60.00-70.00
68. Left	1960's	America	7"	27.00-35.00
Center	1960's	America	8½"	70.00-80.00
Right	1960's	America	7"	70.00-80.00
69. Left	1920-1950's	America	4"	35.00-40.00
Center	1920-1950's	Japan	5" long	85.00-100.00
Right	1920-1950's	Japan	4"	50.00-60.00
70. Left	1920-1940's		5"	40.00-50.00
Center	1920-1940's		1½"	25.00-35.00
Right	1920-1940's		4¾" long	60.00-70.00
71. Left	1920-1940's	Japan	4"	40.00-50.00
Center	1920-1940's	America	9" long	80.00-100.00
Right	1920-1940's	Japan	4"	40.00-50.00
72.	1950's	Japan	3½" long	80.00-90.00
73.			10"	40.00-50.00
74. Top left		America	4¼" long	40.00-50.00
Top right			4½" long	40.00-50.00
Bottom left		America	3½" long	30.00-40.00
Bottom right		Japan	6½" long	40.00-50.00
75. Top	1950's	Occ. Japan	5¼" long	50.00-60.00
Bottom	1950's		10" long	50.00-60.00
76. Left			3¼"	50.00-60.00
Center			3¼"	40.00-45.00
Right			3½"	50.00-60.00
77. Top left			3¼"	50.00-60.00
Top right			3¾"	60.00-70.00
Center		America	3¼"	30.00-40.00
Bottom left		Japan	4"	70.00-80.00
Bottom right		Japan	4¼"	70.00-80.00
78.			10½" long	65.00-75.00
79.			11"	35.00-40.00
80.	1920's		6' long	100.00-125.00
81. Left	1960's	Sweden	8½"	50.00-60.00
Right	1960's-1980's		12"	30.00-35.00
82.	1940's-1950's	America	11½"	60.00-75.00
83. Lg. Reindeer	1950's	W. Germany	10" long	90.00-125.00

Plate No.		Date	Country	Size	Price
	Sm. Reindeer	1950's	W. Germany	6" long	80.00-90.00
	Santa	1950's	W. Germany	8½"	200.00-250.00
84.		1950's	America	7½"	25.00-30.00
85.				11"	25.00-30.00
86.	Left	1950's		12"	40.00-50.00
	Right	1940's-1950's		12½"	50.00-55.00
87.		1960's		7"	20.00-25.00
88.				8"	25.00-35.00
89.				19"	145.00-165.00
90.				26"	160.00-200.00
91.	Left	1960's	Japan	6" long	15.00-18.00
	Center	1960's	Japan	6½"	18.00-22.00
	Right	1960's	Japan	6½"	18.00-20.00
92.	Left	1950's-1960's	America	17"	50.00-75.00
	Right				75.00-125.00
93.	Left		America	11½"	10.00-12.00
	Right		America	8½"	8.00-10.00
94.			Czechoslavakia	7¼"	20.00-25.00
95.		1950's		13"	40.00-45.00
96.	Left			15½"	28.00-32.00
	Right			17"	30.00-35.00
97.	Left	1950's-1960's		13"	15.00-18.00
	Right	1950's-1960's		11"	15.00-18.00

Artificial Trees

Increased collector interest in old figural ornaments and lights has rekindled interest in old artificial trees. Ornament collectors have found the old goose-feather trees with their widely spaced branches present excellent sites for displaying their treasures. As a result, demand for these trees has increased dramatically, and the prices have sky-rocketed.

Generally, prices on feather trees are determined by size, color, condition, and age. Usually the larger the tree the higher the price. Older trees in good condition are the most desirable. Colors other than green are not easily found. White is probably the second most common color. Other colors such as blue, pink, silver, and gold exist. These colors are normally priced only slightly higher than a green tree of equal size, since there is more demand for the green ones. Care should be taken when handlng these trees. Their feathers are easily lost, and they are also damaged by moisture. Few collectors are willing to pay a premium price for trees that have few feathers or are otherwise damaged.

Reproduction feather trees are currently being made. They are not cheap and some are being passed at shows and flea markets as old. Examine trees carefully before buying them. Look for tell-tale signs of age in the paper wrapping around the trunk. Also, check the base the tree is mounted on to make sure the wood is old.

Plate No.		Color	Size	Compostion	Date	Price
98.		green	36"	goose-feather	early 1900's	200.00-250.00
99.	Left	green	26"	goose-feather	1920's-1930's	145.00-185.00
	Center	lt green	22"	goose-feather	early 1900's	145.00-185.00
	Right	green	27"	goose-feather	circa 1900	200.00-250.00
100.	Left	green	38"	goose-feather	1930's	250.00-300.00
	Right	green	37"	goose-feather	1920-1930's	225.00-275.00
101.	Left	green	29"	goose-feather	early 1900's	200.00-250.00
	Right	green	27"	goose-feather	1920-1930's	185.00-200.00
102.	Left	white	25"	goose-feather	1930's	150.00-175.00
	Right	white	32"	goose-feather	1930's	200.00-250.00
103.		green	26"	goose-feather	1930's	150.00-200.00
104.	Left	green	16"	goose-feather	early 1900's	75.00-95.00
	Right	green	19"	goose-feather	early 1900's	65.00-75.00
105.		green	44"	goose-feather	early 1900's	600.00-800.00
106.		teal	72"	goose-feather	1920's-1930's	500.00-600.00
107.		purple	44"	goose-feather	1930's	450.00-500.00
108.	Left	green	11"	goose-feather		50.00-65.00
	Right	green	6"	goose-feather		50.00-65.00
109.	Left	green	5"	goose-feather		60.00-70.00
	Center	green	6½"	goose-feather and paper		45.00-55.00

Plate No.	Color	Size	Composition	Date	Price
Right	green	6"	goose-feather and paper		45.00-55.00
110. Left	green		vinyl	1950's & later	25.00-30.00
Right	green		vinyl	1950's & later	25.00-30.00
111.	pink	9"	rayon	1960's	40.00-45.00
112. Left	green	6"	coated cloth	1930's	20.00-22.00
Right	green	9½"	coated cloth	1930's	25.00-28.00
113. Left	green	10½"	wire		25.00-28.00
Right	green	7½"	tinsel wire		25.00-28.00
114. Left	green	13"	vinyl	1960's & later	18.00-20.00
Right		19"	vinyl	1960's & later	25.00-30.00
115. Left		8"			30.00-35.00
Left center		10"			10.00-15.00
Center		13"			18.00-20.00
Right center	green	10"			10.00-15.00
Right		10½"			25.00-30.00
116.		2" – 5"			2.00-4.00
	green	6" – 9"			5.00-6.00
	green	10" – 14"			14.00-18.00
117.	green	19"	cellophane	1950's	60.00-75.00
118.	green	19"	vinyl	1960's & later	20.00-25.00
119.		23"	cloth	1950's	65.00-75.00
120.		18"	aluminum	1960's	20.00-25.00

Glass Ornaments

Glass Christmas tree ornaments are becoming increasingly collectible as more people are becoming aware of these artistic creations. Most ornaments are priced according to condition, size, subject matter, rarity, and possibly age.

Condition is extremely important in determing the price of an ornament. The ornament should not be cracked or have much silver or paint missing. These conditions will drastically lower the price of an ornament. Any common ornament in poor condition would be almost worthless. Some collectors are willing to accept moderate damage on rarer ornaments.

Most ornaments were made in more than one size. For convenience, and to aid in the pricing of other sizes of ornaments, many of the sizes of the ornaments pictured are listed. Generally, larger size ornaments are more desirable and will be priced higher.

Subject matter also contributes to pricing strategy. Some types of ornaments such as birds, houses, fish, and instruments were made in great numbers. There are plenty of these categories of ornaments. Santa figurals are plentiful, but they are also very popular among collectors. Prices for shapes which are appealing to collectors are continuously rising.

Rarity of glass ornaments is hard to determine. This field of collecting is still too new to ascertain rarity with any meaurable accuracy. Countless numbers of glass ornaments are still being discovered in long-forgotten corners of attics. While many of these discoveries are not yielding anything noteworthy, some treasures are sure to be found. It is always interesting to see which rare items can withstand the tests of time and increased knowledge. Until then, individual collectors will have to draw on their own experience regarding rarity.

Age of an ornament is usually an important condition for pricing. Many ornaments were made over a very long period of time, and the earlier ornaments are usually higher priced. Figural ornaments made before World War I are exspecially desirable

In recent years reproductions of old ornaments have become an increasingly significant problem for collectors. Basically, ornaments may be divided into three different age groups. They are as follows: 1. Ornaments produced before World War II; 2. Ornaments produced during the 1950's and 1960's; 3. Current production of ornaments made from old molds. The early ornaments made before World War II are the most collectible and the highest priced. Ornaments made during the 1950's and 1960's are now being accepted by some collectors at reasonable prices.

Collectors who are willing to spend large sums of money on ornaments need to be well informed about what is currently being made. They also need to know how to differentiate between old and new ornaments. One of the most significant differences between old and new ornaments is in the weight of the glass. Older ornaments are normally lightweight and have very thin wall. The condition of the ornament is also a very good indicator of age. Most of the pre-war ornaments are no longer bright and shiny, although many may still be in excellent condition. The condition and compostion of the metal cap may also indicate age. Most early caps were made of tin or steel, which will often show signs of corrosion. Later caps are often stamped and may be made from foil. However, collectors should also remember that caps are easily replaced. Finally, some collectors resort to a taste test to help them determine the age of an ornament. Due to the nature of the chemicals used in the finishes, ornaments made before World War II often taste salty to the tongue.

Prices indicated below are for the ornaments produced during the time period listed in the 'Date' column. Caution should be excercised when purchasing any of the Italian figurals or Czechoslavakian beaded ornaments. Many of them are still in current production.

Plate No.	Size	Date	Price	Plate No.	Size	Date	Price
121. Kugel, small	2" – 5"	late 1800's	25.00-50.00	Gendarme, right	3"	circa 1930's	35.00-40.00
Kugel, med.	6" – 9"	late 1800's	60.00-100.00	148. Jester head, left	4½"	circa 1960's	25.00-35.00
Kugel, large	over 10"	late 1800's	100.00-150.00	Clown with banjo	4½"	circa 1960's	35.00-40.00
122. Kugel, textured	4½"	late 1800's	200.00-225.00	Clown head, right	3½"	1920's	60.00-70.00
Kugel, red	3½"	late 1800's	40.00-50.00	149. Head, Christ	2½"	pre 1940	75.00-85.00
Kugel, purple	3"	late 1800's	35.00-45.00	Girl, center	3"	circa 1920's	85.00-95.00
123. Kugel, oval	6"	late 1800's	75.00-85.00	Girl, right	2¾"	circa 1920's	85.00-95.00
Kugel, oval	7"	late 1800's	75.00-85.00	150. Head, left	3¾"	pre 1940	50.00-60.00
124. Witch's eye	3½"	early 1900's	75.00-85.00	Indian bust	3½"	1920's	225.00-295.00
125. Imitation Japan	1⅛"		18.00-20.00	151. Scowling Indian	3"	pre 1940	200.00-250.00
kugel				Indian w/warpaint	3½"	pre 1940	225.00-275.00
126. Grape cluster	7½"	early 1900's	185.00-200.00	Indian w/draped	3½"	1920's	250.00-350.00
Grape cluster	2¾"	early 1900's	90.00-110.00	bust			
Grape cluster	6"	early 1900's	100.00-150.00	Indian in a canoe	4"	pre 1940	225.00-295.00
Grape cluster	4½"	early 1900's	100.00-125.00	Scowling Indian on	3"	pre 1940	200.00-250.00
127. American figural	2¼"	early 1900's	75.00-85.00	clip			
128. Glass shade clip	3"	early 1900's	50.00-70.00	152. Indian w/candle	4"	early 1900's	250.00-300.00
129. Glass shade clip	3"	early 1900's	150.00-175.00	clip			
130. Glass shade clip	3½"	early 1900's	75.00-85.00	153. Potato head man	3"	early 1900's	150.00-175.00
131. Bear/extended	3"	1900-1920	175.00-200.00	Smiling face on	3"	1920's-1930's	100.00-125.00
legs				mushroom			
Happy Hooligan	4"	1900-1920	200.00-250.00	154. Ringmaster head	4"	pre 1940	130.00-160.00
132. Palmer Cox	5"	early 1900's	200.00-225.00	Devil head	4"	pre 1940	250.00-275.00
Brownie				Charlie Chaplin	3¾"	pre 1940	250.00-275.00
133. Foxy Grandpa	4½"	early 1900's	225.00-275.00	155. Baby Jesus head	3"	pre 1940	75.00-85.00
Keystone Cop	4¾"	early 1900's	200.00-225.00	Kite head	4½"	early 1900's	200.00-250.00
134. Legless Foxy	5"	early 1900's	275.00-350.00	Girl head	2½"	pre 1940	75.00-85.00
Grandpa				Barney Google	2¾"	pre 1940	200.00-300.00
135. Jockey pipe	5¾""	early 1900's	125.00-150.00	156. Chinaman head on	4¾"	pre 1940	250.00-300.00
136. Skeezix	4¾"	1920's-1930's	200.00-225.00	clip			
137. Lady Liberty	6½"	1920's	125.00-175.00	Pumpkin head on	4¾"	pre 1940	250.00-275.00
138. North Wind	3¾"	early 1920's	90.00-110.00	clip			
blowing				Popcorn head on	4¾"	pre 1940	250.00-300.00
139. Man in the Moon	4¾"	1920's-1930's	75.00-85.00	clip			
Man in the Moon	3½"	1920's-1930's	75.00-85.00	157. Clown head, left	3½"	pre 1940	40.00-45.00
140. Man on moon	2"	1920's-1930's	45.00-60.00	Clown head, center	3"	pre 1940	45.00-50.00
Man playing	6½"	early 1900's	80.00-90.00	Clown head, right	3"	1930's	40.00-45.00
mandolin				158. Clown w/conical	6½"	pre 1940	50.00-65.00
141. Piked head	4½"	early 1900's	150.00-175.00	body			
142. Left	3¾"	pre 1940	85.00-100.00	Embossed juggler	2¾"	pre 1940	40.00-45.00
Right	3½"	pre 1940	60.00-70.00	Clown head/ruffled	4"	pre 1940	30.00-40.00
143. Grapemen	2¼"	early 1900's	125.00-140.00	collar			
Doll head, center	2¼"	1930's-1940's	70.00-85.00	Pink unsilvered	4¼"	pre 1940	100.00-150.00
Doll face, right	1¼"	1920's-1930's	100.00-150.00	clown			
144. Girl/silver hair	4"	pre 1940	90.00-110.00	Common shape	4½"	1930's-1950's	25.00-35.00
Doll head/red cap	3"	pre 1940	100.00-125.00	clown			
Sailor	4"	pre 1940	185.00-225.00	159. Coco the Clown	1½"	1920's	90.00-100.00
Cherub/blond hair	3"	pre 1940	90.00-100.00	Chubby clown	4"	1920's	40.00-50.00
Doll face/blue cap	3¼"	pre 1940	85.00-100.00	160. American clown		pre 1940	35.00-40.00
145. Man in cone, left	3½"	pre 1940	70.00-75.00	Common clowns		1920's-1930's	25.00-35.00
Father Christmas	2½"	1920's-1950's	45.00-50.00	161. Clown, 500,000		pre 1940	90.00-100.00
Man in cone, right	3"	pre 1940	55.00-65.00	162. Clown on moon	3½"	early 1900's	75.00-85.00
146. Elf head	2¾"	1920's	25.00-35.00	Clown, 500,000	4¼"	pre 1940	100.00-125.00
Elf in house	3½"	1920's	45.00-65.00	163. Bell-shaped Jester	3¼"	pre 1940	125.00-150.00
Elf treehouse	3"	1920's	50.00-60.00	164. Jester	3½"	pre 1940	150.00-175.00
147. Girl head, left	3"	circa 1930's	55.00-85.00	165. Punch and Judy	3"	early 1900's	80.00-90.00
Clown head, center	3½"	pre 1940	50.00-60.00	166. Hansel	3¾"	pre 1940	90.00-100.00

Plate No.	Size	Date	Price
Gretel	3¾"	pre 1940	100.00-110.00
167. Moses in a basket	3¼"	pre 1940	75.00-95.00
168. Baby	2¾"	pre 1940	90.00-110.00
169. Baby with pacifier	2½"	early 1900's	90.00-100.00
170. Little boy on sled	4"	early 1900's	100.00-125.00
171. Baby in blanket	3¼"	early 1900's	70.00-90.00
Snowbaby	4"	1920's	80.00-90.00
Little Miss Muffet	4"	1920's	75.00-85.00
172. Ali Baba	4"	pre 1940	125.00-150.00
173. Witch		pre 1940	200.00-225.00
174. Red Riding Hood	3"	early 1900's	100.00-125.00
175. Boy/accordian	3¾"	1920's	45.00-55.00
German boy	3½"	1920's	60.00-65.00
Goldilocks	3½"	1930's	75.00-85.00
176. Begger Man	3"	1920's	75.00-90.00
177. Policeman	4½"	pre 1940	125.00-150.00
Hessian soldier	5¼"	pre 1940	150.00-175.00
Baby Aviator	5"	pre 1940	200.00-250.00
178. Butcher/baker	3¾"	pre 1940	80.00-90.00
Girl in flower basket	3¼"	pre 1940	35.00-45.00
Dutch boy	4½"	pre 1940	75.00-85.00
Girl w/spoon/carrot	3¾"	pre 1940	50.00-60.00
179. Patriotic lady	3"	pre 1940	60.00-75.00
Mrs. Santa Claus	3½"	1920's	90.00-110.00
180. Girl face in flower	2½"	pre 1940	25.00-35.00
Girl face in flower w/candle clip	3¾"	pre 1940	45.00-55.00
181. Tree top angel	5"	pre 1940	100.00-125.00
182. Pincushion girl	4¼"	pre 1940	75.00-100.00
Girl in a flower	3½"	pre 1940	100.00-125.00
Choir girl	3½"	pre 1940	80.00-90.00
Kate Greenaway girl	4½"	pre 1940	125.00-150.00
Angel	3½"	pre 1940	50.00-65.00
183. Angel/scrap face	3½"	circa 1900	95.00-110.00
184. Angel w/Dresden wings	4½"	pre 1940	125.00-175.00
Angel on silver ball	5"	pre 1940	150.00-185.00
185. Snowman on clip	3¾"	pre 1940	70.00-80.00
Angel w/Dresden wings	4" 3	pre 1940	125.00-175.00
186. Snowman, left	½"	1950's	20.00-25.00
Snowman, center	3½"	1930's	25.00-30.00
Snowman, right	3½"	1950's	20.00-25.00
Beggarman	3½"	early 1900's	40.00-50.00
187. Snowman in chimney	4"	pre 1940	90.00-110.00
Snowman on white ball	5"	pre 1940	75.00-80.00
Snowman on ball w/silver net	4½"	pre 1940	75.00-80.00
188. Santa, left	3"	1920's-1930's	25.00-35.00
Santa, left center	3"	1920's-1930's	25.00-35.00
Santa, right center	3"	1920's-1930's	25.00-35.00
Santa head	5"	1950's	60.00-65.00
189. Santa, left	3½"	1920's	35.00-45.00
Santa, right	3"	1930's	35.00-45.00
190. Santa on ball	3¾"	1920's-1930's	35.00-45.00
Santa with tree	3¼"	1920's-1930's	25.00-30.00
Santa with basket	3½"	1920's	35.00-45.00
191. Santa, left	3"	1930's	40.00-45.00
Santa, center	3½"	1920's	45.00-55.00
Santa, right	4½"	1920's-1930's	35.00-45.00
192. Santa w/gold bag	3⅜"	pre 1940	35.00-45.00
Santa w/white tree	4¼"	pre 1940	75.00-85.00
Santa on clip	3¾"	pre 1940	85.00-90.00
Red/silver Santa	3¾"	pre 1940	35.00-45.00

Plate No.	Size	Date	Price
Santa w/long beard	5½"	pre 1940	100.00-150.00
193. Santa w/scrap face	4¼"	pre 1940	100.00-150.00
Santa w/glass eyes	5"	pre 1940	150.00-200.00
Santa w/wire legs	5"	pre 1940	100.00-125.00
194. Santa, left	3¾"	1930's	25.00-30.00
Santa on clip	6"	1920's	125.00-150.00
195. Gold Santa	3½"	early 1900's	40.00-45.00
Silver Santa	3½"	early 1900's	40.00-45.00
196. Santa w/basket	4"	1920's-1930's	35.00-45.00
197. Tree top Santa	4¼"	pre 1940	100.00-125.00
198. Bell w/embossed Santa	5"	pre 1940	85.00-125.00
Santa on bell	3	pre 1940	100.00-125.00
Blue Santa on bell	½"	pre 1940	80.00-90.00
Angel on bell	5"	pre 1940	80.00-90.00
199. Santa in stocking	3½"	pre 1940	90.00-110.00
Green stocking	4"	pre 1940	80.00-90.00
200. Snow White & Seven Dwarfs set		late 1930's	500.00-600.00
201. Dog with a bow	4"	1920's	85.00-90.00
Cat in shoe	4"	early 1900's	100.00-125.00
Cat in bag	4¼"	1920's	95.00-110.00
202. Two-faced dog	1½"	pre 1940	40.00-45.00
Cat on a clip	2¼"	pre 1940	100.00-150.00
203. Head		pre 1940	85.00-90.00
204. Dog w/ear muffs	3½"	pre 1940	50.00-65.00
Seated Spaniel	3"	pre 1940	50.00-65.00
Blue dog w/trumpet	3½"	pre 1940	60.00-65.00
Sitting dog	4"	pre 1940	65.00-70.00
205. Scotty	4"	1920's	40.00-50.00
Begging dog	3¾"	1900-1930's	50.00-65.00
Dog in bag	3"	1920's-1930's	75.00-85.00
206. Bear with a muff	3¾"	pre 1940	50.00-60.00
Lg bear w/a stick	3¾"	pre 1940	60.00-80.00
Bear in clown suit	4"	pre 1940	85.00-90.00
Sm bear w/a stick	2½"	pre 1940	50.00-55.00
207. Mouse on clip	4"	1920's	75.00-100.00
Dog on ball	3½"	1930's	40.00-45.00
Elephant on ball	2¾"	1920's-1930's	45.00-65.00
208. Pig with flower		pre 1940	60.00-80.00
Monkey		pre 1940	85.00-100.00
Bear with a stick		pre 1940	50.00-60.00
209. Silver pig	5½"	1950's	85.00-100.00
210. Standing elephant	3¼"	late 1800-1920's	100.00-125.00
211. Cat in shoe	3¼"	early 1900's	90.00-100.00
Glass shoe	4¾"	early 1900's	75.00-100.00
212. Radio monkey	4½"	1920's-1930's	150.00-180.00
213. Embossed rabbit	2¾"	pre 1940	50.00-60.00
Pig	4"	pre 1940	100.00-150.00
Chick on nest	3"	pre 1940	100.00-125.00
214. Squirrel with a nut	2½"	pre 1940	60.00-80.00
Rabbit with a carrot	4"	pre 1940	85.00-100.00
215. Fox	3"		40.00-50.00
Deer	2½"		40.00-50.00
216. Sm silver deer	3½"		20.00-25.00
Lg silver deer	6"		65.00-75.00
Gold deer	5¼"		55.00-65.00
217. Blown deer	5"	circa 1930's	45.00-55.00
218. Parrot, large		pre 1940	40.00-45.00
Common birds on clips		1920's-1930's	12.00-18.00
White bird		pre 1940	30.00-40.00
219. Parrot		1920's-1950's	18.00-20.00
Turkey		pre 1940	18.00-20.00
Hummingbird		pre 1940	20.00-25.00
220. Peacock	4"	pre 1940	18.00-20.00

Plate No.	Size	Date	Price
Chick	3"	pre 1940	40.00-50.00
Birds on nest	3½"	pre 1940	45.00-55.00
221. Peacock, left		1920's-1950's	25.00-30.00
Peacock, right		pre 1940	20.00-22.00
222. Owls		1920's-1930's	30.00-40.00
223. Bird, left	2¾"	1920's	40.00-50.00
Bird, center	2¼"	1920's	30.00-35.00
Bird, right	2¼"	1920's	35.00-45.00
224. Bird, left	2"	early 1900's	30.00-35.00
Bird, right	3"	early 1900's	40.00-45.00
225. Duck	3"	pre 1940	60.00-80.00
Embossed turkey	3"	pre 1940	50.00-55.00
Embossed turkey	2½"	pre 1940	40.00-50.00
226. Embossed parrot	3"	pre 1940	30.00-35.00
Eagle	3½"	pre 1940	90.00-100.00
227. Birdcages w/ embossed birds		pre 1940	30.00-50.00
228. Carousels w/ animals		pre 1940	30.00-40.00
229. Twin storks	4"	pre 1940	30.00-40.00
Stork w/closed beak	5½"	pre 1940	30.00-35.00
Stork w/open beak	6"	pre 1940	30.00-40.00
Twin canaries	7"	pre 1940	30.00-40.00
230. Crane w/blue body	4½"	pre 1940	40.00-50.00
Crane w/silver body	5¾"	pre 1940	35.00-45.00
231. Snake	7"	1890's-1930's	100.00-125.00
232. Goldfish	4" – 4½"	1890's-1930's	35.00-40.00
233. Fish		1920's-1950's	30.00-40.00
Fish, wire-wrapped		pre 1940	20.00-25.00
234. Shark	7"	pre 1940	100.00-150.00
Seahorse	4½"	pre 1940	100.00-150.00
235. Puffer	2½"	pre 1940	30.00-40.00
Angel fish	2" – 4"	pre 1940	30.00-60.00
Shark	4"	pre 1940	20.00-25.00
Fish with waves	5"	pre 1940	35.00-45.00
236. Anchor	5½"	pre 1940	25.00-35.00
Boat		pre 1940	125.00-140.00
Mermaid	4¼"	pre 1940	125.00-140.00
237. Regular frog	4"	pre 1940	80.00-90.00
Singing frog	3¾"	pre 1940	150.00-175.00
238. Pearl in shell	3"	pre 1940	85.00-90.00
239. Frog on a ball	5½"	1920's	90.00-125.00
240. Beetle on flower	3"	pre 1940	55.00-65.00
241. Embossed butterfly	2½"	pre 1940	45.00-55.00
Embossed beetle	2¼"	pre 1940	50.00-60.00
Embossed butterfly	2½"	pre 1940	45.00-55.00
242. Butterfly, left	2¼"	pre 1940	30.00-40.00
Scarab, center	2¾"	early 1900's	75.00-80.00
Moth, right	2¼"	early 1900's	30.00-40.00
243. Moth, left	2¼"	early 1900's	120.00-140.00
Moth, center	2¼"	pre 1940	120.00-140.00
Moth, right	3½"	pre 1940	150.00-190.00
244. Butterfly	2½"	pre 1940	100.00-110.00
245. Green butterfly	3½"	pre 1940	140.00-180.00
Yellow butterfly	3"	pre 1940	150.00-175.00
246. Red/yellow rose	3½"	pre 1940	70.00-80.00
Lg trumpet flower	4"	pre 1940	70.00-80.00
Sm trumpet flower	2½"	pre 1940	40.00-45.00
247. Textured flower	3¾"	pre 1940	70.00-80.00
Unsilvered flower bud	3"	early 1900's	35.00-40.00
Glass shade	3"	early 1900's	40.00-45.00
248. Top left		early 1900's	32.00-35.00
Center left		pre 1940	32.00-35.00
Bottom left		pre 1940	70.00-80.00
Glass shade clip		pre 1940	50.00-60.00

Plate No.	Size	Date	Price
249. Rose candle clip		pre 1940	60.00-80.00
Silver flower		pre 1940	50.00-60.00
Flower candle clip		pre 1940	65.00-85.00
250. Trumpet flower	3¼"	pre 1940	65.00-85.00
Ornament w/cloth flowers	2½"	pre 1940	50.00-60.00
251. Red rose	2½"	pre 1940	20.00-25.00
252. Banana	4½"	early 1900's	75.00-85.00
Watermelon slice	5½"	1900-1930's	100.00-125.00
253. Acorns	2¼"	pre 1940	25.00-30.00
Rose	3¼"	pre 1940	40.00-50.00
Cherries	3¼"	pre 1940	35.00-40.00
Grape cluster	3¾"	pre 1940	35.00-40.00
254. Embossed cherries/ 3-sided	3½"	pre 1940	35.00-45.00
Embossed cherries	4"	pre 1940	20.00-25.00
Cherry w/leaves	3¾"	pre 1940	15.00-18.00
255. Red fruit cluster	3"	pre 1940	85.00-100.00
Pineapple	3½"	pre 1940	25.00-30.00
Strawberry	2"	pre 1940	20.00-25.00
Radish	3¾"	pre 1940	20.00-25.00
Peach	3½"	pre 1940	20.00-25.00
Strawberry	2½"	pre 1940	18.00-20.00
Unsilvered banana	4"	pre 1940	65.00-75.00
256. Miniature fruit	1¾" – 2¼"	pre 1940	18.00-20.00
257. Orange	2"	1920's	22.00-32.00
Peach	3¾"	1920's-1930's	22.00-32.00
Lemon	4"	1920's	30.00-35.00
258. Pear	4"	1900-1930's	30.00-35.00
Tomato	2¾"	1900-1920's	50.00-60.00
Strawberry	3¼"	1920's	35.00-45.00
259. Fruit w/candle clips		pre 1940	35.00-55.00
260. Orange, left	2½"	pre 1940	20.00-30.00
Tomato	2¼"	pre 1940	20.00-30.00
Orange, right	3½"	pre 1940	20.00-30.00
261. Fruit w/candle clips		pre 1940	30.00-35.00
262. Cone	6"	pre 1940	50.00-60.00
Cornucopia	4"	pre 1940	45.00-55.00
Flower basket		pre 1940	20.00-25.00
Fruit basket		pre 1940	20.00-25.00
263. Grapes, wire-wrapped	4¼"	early 1900-1930's	10.00-18.00
Pinecone, wire-wrapped	3½"	early 1900's	10.00-18.00
264. Grape cluster, left	3½"	1950's	12.00-14.00
Grape cluster, right	3½"	1920's-1930's	20.00-25.00
265. Berry cluster	3¾"	pre 1940	20.00-22.00
Berry cluster	3"	pre 1940	20.00-22.00
Peas in a pod	3"	pre 1940	30.00-40.00
Strawberry	2"	pre 1940	25.00-30.00
266. Carrot	3½"	1920's-1930's	55.00-70.00
Ear of corn	3½"	1900-1930's	40.00-50.00
Pickle	4"	1900-1930's	80.00-100.00
267. Potato	3¼"	pre 1940	100.00-125.00
Ear of corn	5"	pre 1940	45.00-50.00
Squash	3½"	pre 1940	45.00-55.00
268. Indian corn	2"	pre 1940	45.00-55.00
269. Triple mushroom	4¼"	pre 1940	50.00-55.00
Single mushroom	3½"	pre 1940	30.00-35.00
Lg. mushroom/2 sm mushroom	2½"	pre 1940	45.00-55.00
270. Single mushroom		pre 1940	27.00-30.00
271. Acorn		pre 1940	8.00-11.00

Plate No.	Size	Date	Price		Plate No.	Size	Date	Price
Walnut, amall		pre 1940	8.00-11.00		296. Pocket watch	2"	pre 1940	35.00-45.00
Walnut, large		pre 1940	15.00-18.00		Cuckoo clock	3½"	pre 1940	45.00-65.00
272. Pinecone		pre 1940	8.00-11.00		297. Bells		pre 1940	20.00-40.00
273. Left		pre 1940	35.00-37.00		298. Teapot		pre 1940	12.00-20.00
Right	4½"	pre 1940	20.00-25.00		Sugar		pre 1940	12.00-20.00
274. Pine tree	4½"	1920's-1930's	30.00-35.00		299. Gold teapot	2½"	pre 1940	25.00-30.00
Pine, decorated	4"	1920's-1930's	35.00-40.00		Pink teapot	2½"	pre 1940	20.00-25.00
275. Gold Christmas tree	3½"	pre 1940	25.00-30.00		Silver teapot	2"	pre 1940	20.00-22.00
Red Christmas tree	4½"	pre 1940	40.00-45.00		300. Montgomery Ward		1940's-1950's	18.00-20.00
276. Horn	4¾"	pre 1940	12.00-14.00		teapots			
Pipe	4½"	pre 1940	15.00-18.00		301. Embossed rope	3¾"	pre 1940	25.00-30.00
277. Lyre	6½"	1920's-1930's	30.00-35.00		Embossed cherubs	4¼"	pre 1940	40.00-45.00
Horn, top	4"	pre 1940	20.00-22.00		Embossed flowers	3¼"	pre 1940	35.00-40.00
Guitar	3¾"	1920's-1930's	12.00-15.00		302. Lamp, left		pre 1940	15.00-18.00
Horn, bottom	2½"	pre 1940	10.00-12.00		Lamp, left center		pre 1940	15.00-18.00
278. Drum	6"	pre 1940	20.00-25.00		Lamp, right center		pre 1940	25.00-30.00
Horn	5¾"	pre 1940	25.00-30.00		Lamp, right		pre 1940	25.00-30.00
Cello	4½"	pre 1940	15.00-18.00		303. Miniature basket	1"	1950's	10.00-12.00
279. Arms w/scrap Santa	5"	pre 1940	30.00-40.00		304. Floral purse	2½"	pre 1940	50.00-80.00
Arms w/hand		pre 1940	45.00-55.00		Money bag – 50000	2¾"	pre 1940	50.00-70.00
Arms w/Dresden	3½"	pre 1940	80.00-90.00		305. Dice candle clip	2½"	pre 1940	50.00-60.00
butterfly					306. Telephone	2"	1940's	60.00-70.00
280. Ocean liner	2¾"	pre 1940	50.00-60.00		307. Football		early 1900's	100.00-125.00
Automobile	3½"	pre 1940	125.00-150.00		308. Candle	3½"	1940's	18.00-20.00
Square-shape car	2¼"	pre 1940	110.00-125.00		309. Icicle	14"	1950's	25.00-35.00
281. Roadster	3"	pre 1940	110.00-125.00		310. Icicle	5"		12.00-15.00
282. Sedan	3¼"	pre 1940	125.00-140.00		311. Candy cane		pre 1960	8.00-10.00
Early coupe		pre 1940	125.00-150.00		312. Beaded ornament		1950's	20.00-25.00
283. Red coupe	3¼"	pre 1940	125.00-150.00		Occupied Japan			
"Funny car"	3¼"	pre 1940	150.00-175.00		313. Beaded ornament		pre 1960	22.00-30.00
Blue sedan	3¼"	pre 1940	125.00-150.00		Czech			
284. Graff Zeppelin	5"	1920's	200.00-250.00		Pacifier		pre 1940	35.00-45.00
Steamship	4"	early 1900's	125.00-140.00		314. Beaded ornament		pre 1960	30.00-35.00
285. Zeppelin "Los Ange-		1920's	175.00-200.00		Czech			
les"					315. Beaded ornament		pre 1960	18.00-22.00
286. Zeppelin "ZR-3"		1920's	200.00-225.00		Czech	7½"		
287. Zeppelin		pre 1940	175.00-200.00		316. Bell		1950's	6.00-8.00
288. Pipe, bent Dublin	5"	early 1900's	60.00-80.00		317. String garland		1950's	10.00-12.00
Pipe	4"	circa 1930's	20.00-25.00		beads, Japan			
289. Shoe	4¾"	pre 1940	85.00-100.00		318. Garland string	28"	1920's-1930's	25.00-30.00
290. Church	4¼"	1920's	18.00-20.00		319. Garland string	60"	1920's-1930's	30.00-35.00
Cottage, center	3¾"	1900-1930's	15.00-18.00		320. Garland string	36"	1920's-1930's	25.00-30.00
Cottage, right	3¾"	1900-1930's	25.00-30.00		321. Garland string	24"	1920's-1930's	30.00-35.00
291. Embossed houses		pre 1940	20.00-50.00		322. Hanging ornament	8"–12"	1920's-1930's	15.00-20.00
Embossed windmill		pre 1940	30.00-45.00		323. Hanging ornament	12"	pre 1960	25.00-30.00
on bell					324. Garland string	110"	1950's	20.00-25.00
292. Tower w/silver top	4¼"	pre 1940	40.00-50.00		325. Garland string	110"	1950's	20.00-25.00
Tower w/snow top	4"	pre 1940	20.00-25.00		326. Italian figural	6"	1950's-1970's	20.00-22.00
293. Windmill	3"	1920's	25.00-30.00		327. Italian figural	6"	1950's-1970's	25.00-28.00
Guardhouse	3"	1920's-1930's	30.00-35.00		328. Italian figural	6"	1950's-1970's	25.00-30.00
Lighthouse	3½"	1920's-1930's	30.00-35.00		329. Italian spaceman	6"	1950's-1970's	30.00-40.00
294. Outhouse	5½"	pre 1940	35.00-45.00		Italian spaceship	5½"	1950's-1970's	30.00-35.00
Lighthouse	4"	pre 1940	35.00-40.00		330. Italian helicopter	8"	1950's-1970's	50.00-55.00
295. Candle on a clip	5"	pre 1940	100.00-125.00		331. Mouse			45.00-55.00

Wire-Wrapped Ornaments

The wire wrapping on these glass ornaments is easily damaged. As a result, many wire-wrapped ornaments are found without much of their wire. Early Victorian wire-wrapped unsilvered ornaments are the most desirable and the highest priced. Later wire-wrapped ornaments were made in the 1920's and 1930's. Many of these ornaments were silvered. Some shapes such as bells, sailboats, umbrellas, and swans are common.

Plate No.	Size	Price		Plate No.	Size	Price
332. Balloon w/scrap decoration	6½"	60.00-70.00		341. Birdcage	9"	125.00-145.00
333. Ball and scrap		60.00-80.00		Bird on nest	4"	65.00-75.00
Sailboat		65.00-80.00		342. Bell	4" – 5½"	40.00-50.00
334. Angel on ball		30.00-35.00		343. Swan	4"	25.00-35.00
Gondola		35.00-45.00		344. Chandelier	5"	125.00-140.00
335. Blue airplane w/scrap Santa	6¼"	60.00-80.00		Multi-arm ornament	6"	90.00-100.00
Red airplane w/scrap Santa	7"	60.00-80.00		345. Mandolin	4" – 5"	40.00-45.00
336. Sailboats	5" – 6"	55.00-65.00		346. Flowerpot	5"	20.00-30.00
337. Steamship	5"	55.00-60.00		Vase	6"	25.00-35.00
Fruit cornucopia	6½"	60.00-80.00		347. Horn		75.00-95.00
Dirgible w/scrap Santa face	4"	75.00-85.00		Violin		65.00-85.00
338. Spider		125.00-150.00		Bottle		60.00-70.00
339. Basket	4"	60.00-70.00		348. Umbrella, open	5½"	30.00-32.00
Umbrella	4"	35.00-45.00		Umbrella, closed	9¼"	25.00-35.00
340. Umbrella		85.00-100.00		Santa on ball	7"	25.00-28.00

Glass and Tinsel Ornaments

Plate No.	Size	Price		Plate No.	Size	Price
349. Left		70.00-75.00		351. Left	9"	25.00-27.00
Right		90.00-100.00		Right	7"	25.00-27.00
350. Left		35.00-40.00		352. Santa scrap in glass ornament	5½"	40.00-50.00
Right		65.00-70.00		353. Girl from scrap and glass		40.00-45.00

Scrap and Spun Glass Ornaments

The older and large scrap and spun glass ornaments are gradually increasing in price. Some newer ornaments were made in Western Germany in the late 1940s.

Plate No.	Size	Price		Plate No.	Size	Price
354. Sunburst w/wax baby	5"	50.00-60.00		Angel, right	3"	20.00-25.00
355.	5½"	65.00-78.00		359. Angels	6"	55.00-65.00
356. Father Christmas	9½"	75.00-80.00		360. Santa head		25.00-35.00
357. Father Christmas	7½"	60.00-70.00		Tree top w/Santa figure	8"	55.00-65.00
358. Angel, left	6"	20.00-25.00		361. Girl in wreath	5½"	40.00-45.00
Angel, center	4½"	22.00-25.00		Tree top w/angel scrap	8"	55.00-65.00

Scrap and Tinsel Ornaments

Due to the vast number of conbinations of scraps and tinsel, pricing this category is virtually impossible. In addition to the many styles produced commercially, millions of ornaments were made at home by individuals. To further complicate matters, dealers are now putting together scrap and tinsel to produce ornaments. Generally, scrap and tinsel ornaments with a colored cellophane backing are old. Also, Santa figural ornaments are usually the most desirable.

Plate No.	Size	Price		Plate No.	Size	Price
362. Santa	9"	90.00-110.00		371. Top		30.00-35.00
363. Santa	9"	90.00-110.00		Bottom		40.00-45.00
364. Santa	6"	20.00-25.00		372. Left	7½"	25.00-30.00
365. Children	6"	15.00-20.00		Right	9"	20.00-25.00
366. Children	6"	15.00-20.00		373. Cornucopia	8½"	25.00-35.00
367. Left	6½"	15.00-20.00		Tree top star	9"	45.00-55.00
Right	4"	15.00-20.00		374. Girl w/flag	6"	50.00-60.00
368. Santa		45.00-55.00		Cupid on horseshoe	7"	50.00-60.00
Others	4½" – 6"	15.00-20.00		375. Mandolin	9"	35.00-40.00
369. Children	8"	15.00-20.00		376. Boot		35.00-40.00
370. Key	7½"	40.00-55.00		Cornucopia		25.00-35.00
Shoe	7½"	35.00-40.00				

Cotton Ornaments

Cotton figurals in human and animal forms are very desirable collectibles. The highest priced cotton figurals are from the late 1800's and will have composition faces. Other figures will be found with celluloid or scrap faces. These will usually be less expensive.

Plate No.	Size	Price	Plate No.	Size	Price
377. Flat cut-out	2" – 4"	16.00-20.00	Girl	3½"	150.00-200.00
Flat cut-out	5" – 9"	25.00-30.00	388. Santa, left	3½"	160.00-180.00
Flat cut-out	over 10"	35.00-45.00	Santa, right	3½"	160.00-180.00
378. Peasant girl	17½"	175.00-185.00	389. Left	4"	50.00-70.00
379. Left	9"	130.00-140.00	Right	3½"	50.00-70.00
Right	9"	125.00-140.00	390. Peasant girl	5½"	160.00-190.00
380.	5"	175.00-200.00	Santa	4"	35.00-40.00
381.	5"	150.00-175.00	391. Santa	6"	70.00-90.00
382. Snow figure	4¾"	28.00-32.00	392. Snowman	6"	50.00-55.00
383. Santa, left	5"	35.00-38.00	Girl	3½"	70.00-80.00
Santa, right	6"	40.00-45.00	393.	5"	30.00-35.00
384. Santa, left	7"	35.00-45.00	394.	4¾"	70.00-75.00
Santa, right	7"	35.00-45.00	395. Angel doll	4"	100.00-125.00
385.		35.00-45.00	396. Cotton animals		30.00-35.00
386. Santa	10½"	90.00-110.00	397. Elephant	4½"	60.00-80.00
387. Bear	2½"	200.00-250.00			

Pressed Cotton Ornaments

The most desirable pressed cotton ornaments are the earlier ones which have good detail and excellent color. Many of the fruits and vegetables are common. Some of the harder to find ornaments will have unusual coloring or may be wire-wrapped. The least desirable cotton ornaments are the earlier ones which have been discolored and the later ones which are plain white.

Plate No.	Size	Price	Plate No.	Size	Price
398. Icicle	6"	20.00-25.00	Apple	2½"	20.00-30.00
399. Pear, small	1½"	18.00-20.00	Banana	6½"	80.00-100.00
Orange, small	1"	18.00-20.00	401. Bell	1½"	18.00-20.00
Orange, med.	2½"	25.00-30.00	Icicle	4"	18.00-20.00
Pear, large	3½"	30.00-35.00	Champagne bottle	3"	30.00-40.00
Lemon	3"	30.00-35.00	Snowman	3½"	18.00-20.00
Apple, med.	2"	25.00-30.00	402. Turnip	4"	20.00-22.00
400. Apple, wire-wrapped	2"	30.00-40.00	Pear	3½"	20.00-25.00
Carrot	3"	25.00-30.00	Peach	3"	30.00-35.00
Turnip	2½"	20.00-30.00	Beet	3"	25.00-30.00
Radish	2½"	20.00-30.00			

Paper Ornaments

Traditionally, three-dimensional Dresden paper ornaments have been the most expensive and most sought after Christmas tree ornaments. Although Dresden ornaments are still expensive and still appeal to many collectors, they are starting to lose their elite status in the price category as glass and other types of ornaments are beginning to be appreciated more.

The papier-mache candleholders are rare and are seldom found in good condition.

Plate No.	Size	Date	Price	Plate No.	Size	Date	Price
403. Belsnickle	3½"	circa 1900	225.00-250.00	Rocking horse	2½"		12.00-15.00
Belsnickle	4"	circa 1900	150.00-200.00	Wagon	2¾"		12.00-15.00
404. Candleholder	6"	late 1800's	300.00-400.00	413. Santa on a swing	5"		50.00-65.00
405. Medal, Dresden-type	3" – 3½"		55.00-65.00	414. Package tag	3½"		10.00-12.00
406. Coach, Dresden	6¼"		225.00-300.00	415. Left	7"		12.00-15.00
407. Owl, Dresden	4"		190.00-225.00	Right	5"		14.00-18.00
408. Eagle, Dresden	5½"		225.00-300.00	416. Angel	12"		30.00-40.00
409. Lizard, Dresden	4¼"		195.00-250.00	417.	7"		20.00-35.00
410. Rifle, Dresden	6¼"		200.00-250.00	418. Angel	6"		18.00-20.00
411. Guitar candy container	4"		75.00-95.00	419. House, Czech	1½"		15.00-25.00
412. Drum	2"		12.00-15.00	420. House, cardboard	2¾"		16.00-20.00
Baby buggy	2¼"		12.00-15.00	421. House, cardboard	1¾"		8.00-10.00

Wax Ornaments

Plate No.	Size	Price	Plate No.	Size	Price
422. Angel	11"	225.00-250.00	425. Angel	7"	135.00-145.00
423. Angel, blonde	9"	185.00-225.00	426. Common angels	4"	70.00-90.00
424. Angel	7"	160.00-180.00			

Chenille Ornaments

Chenille ornaments are generally inexpensive and readily available. Special marks such as "Germany" or "Occupied Japan" may add a little value to the ornament.

Plate No.	Size	Price	Plate No.	Size	Price
427. Santa, clay face		25.00-30.00	Wreath		8.00-10.00
Cane	5"	5.00-6.00	430. Bell, left		65.00-75.00
428. Cane	12"	8.00-10.00	Bell, right		20.00-30.00
429. Santa, left		10.00-12.00	431. Figure		15.00-20.00
Santa, Occ. Japan		20.00-22.00			

Celluloid and Plastic

Plate No.	Price	Plate No.	Price
432. Dirgible, celluloid	60.00-80.00	434. Plastic figures	5.00-8.00
433. Bird	40.00-50.00	435. Pixie ornaments	5.00-8.00
Little girl	50.00-55.00	436. Ornament	15.00-18.00
Santa	55.00-60.00		

Metal Ornaments

Soft metal ornaments made from the tin-lead alloys produced before World War I are not easy to find. Many of these ornaments were later melted down. Others which survived the smelter were easily damaged and are hard to find in good shape. Other metal ornaments which are in demand are those made form brass and pewter.

Plate No.	Price	Plate No.	Price
437. Left	20.00-25.00	441. Star	10.00-12.00
Right	20.00-25.00	442. Santa, electric	55.00-60.00
438. Birdcage	25.00-35.00	443. Wood and papier-mache ornament	100.00-150.00
Basket	25.00-35.00		
439. Birdcage	20.00-25.00	444. Horn, brass	55.00-65.00
440. Birdcage, wind-up	150.00-190.00		

Candle Clips and Candleholders

Candleholders and candle clips are an interesting collectible. The more desirable holders are rapidly increasing in price. Top of the line glass jars include those with the Queen's head embossed. Other high priced jars are those in the colors ruby and cobalt. The highest priced candle clips are the double-sided ones with a chromolithographed Father Christmas figure. Other chromolithographed spring clips are close behind. Counterweight holders with extremely fancy weights are also selling briskly at very good prices.

Some common variety spring clip holders are still available in both enameled and plain tin versions. They are being imported from Germany and the Orient and usually sell for around one dollar each.

Plate No.	Size	Date	Price	Plate No.	Size	Date	Price
445. Brass candleholder	2"	1920's	35.00-40.00	Blue milk glass	4"	late 1800's	35.00-45.00
446. Cobalt, left	4"	late 1800's	100.00-125.00	Teal	4"	late 1800's	35.00-40.00
White milk glass with embossed head	4"	late 1800's	150.00-160.00	Amythest	4"	late 1800's	22.00-28.00
				White opal	4"	late 1800's	22.00-27.00
Cobalt, center	4"	late 1800's	100.00-125.00	White milk glass	4"	late 1800's	18.00-22.00
Cranberry	4"	late 1800's	125.00-135.00	448. Fancy weight	6"	late 1800's	30.00-37.00
Cobalt, right with embossed head	4"	late 1800's	150.00-160.00	Ball weight	4"–6"	late 1800's	15.00-18.00
Teal with embossed head	3½"	late 1800's	150.00-200.00	Extension holder	4½"		20.00-22.00
				449. Father Christmas clip	2¼"	early 1900's	100.00-125.00
447. Red	4"	late 1800's	50.00-60.00	450. Clips with angels	1½"	early 1900's	25.00-35.00
Cobalt	4"	late 1800's	40.00-50.00	451. Star-shaped angel	2"	early 1900's	45.00-55.00
Amber	4"	late 1800's	18.00-22.00	Angel, center	3"	early 1900's	50.00-75.00

Plate No.	Size	Date	Price	Plate No.	Size	Date	Price
Cupid on elbows	2½"	early 1900's	45.00-55.00	Butterfly	1"	early 1900's	20.00-25.00
452. Floral candle clip	1½"	early 1900's	30.00-35.00	Butterfly	1¾"	early 1900's	20.00-25.00
453. Top: Angel	3"	early 1900's	85.00-95.00	Bottom: Floral, painted	1½"		5.00-8.00
Father Christmas	2⅜"	early 1900's	50.00-60.00	Unenameled	1¾"		3.00-4.00
Farm scene	2½"		40.00-50.00	Enameled long	2½"		10.00-12.00
Center: Pinecone	2¼"	early 1900's	15.00-20.00	Bird	2¼"	early 1900's	12.00-15.00
Squirrel	2"	early 1900's	20.00-25.00	454. Common clips	1" – 2"		2.00-3.50

Electric Lights

Prices on bulbs are primarily governed by age, desirability, condition, and rarity. Desirability and rarity are in many instances determined by the subject matter of the bulb. Many of the white milk glass Japanese figural lights were produced in great quantities. Characters which were the most popular between the 1920's and the 1950's were made in the largest numbers. These items such as Santa figures, birds, houses, lanterns, and many animals are found most commonly today. Some of the rare and more expensive Japanese lamps are the cartoon characters and special figures which were only made for a short time.

Figural tree lights produced prior to World War I were mostly European. These lights were painted over transparent glass and have a prominent exhaust tip on the figural body. Also, the insulator used in the base of the bulbs made before World War I will usually be either ceramic or ivory. Certain rare very early lights may be found with plaster or paper insulators. Lights made in Japan and elsewhere after 1920 will generally have black glass insulators, and the exhaust point was moved to the base.

Today collectors are paying the highest prices for pre-1920 figurals. Some of the harder-to-find white milk glass Japanese figurals are also creeping up in price. Currently, many collectors are demanding lights which still work, although burned out samples of hard to find lights are sometimes acceptable at reduced prices.

Avon has reproduced a set of seven bulbs from originals in their "Gallery Reproduction Series." Copies were made from bulbs on display at the Ford Museum. There are only five different bulbs in the set, since each set includes two snowmen and two Santa figures. The other three bulbs are a caroler, a lamp, and a ball. The new lights have a C-7 base, were made in Taiwan, and are marked "Taiwan" on the bottom of the base.

Plate No.	Date	Price	Plate No.	Date	Price
455. Empire boxed set	early 1900's	175.00-225.00	Small Father Christmas	circa 1915	35.00-50.00
Porcelain socket string		90.00-100.00	473. Jester	about 1910	130.00-165.00
Carbon filament light		5.00-7.00	Indian	about 1910	350.00-375.00
456. Boxed C-7 set	circa 1915	175.00-225.00	Clown	about 1910	155.00-160.00
457. Ever-Ready set	circa 1910	110.00-130.00	474. Top: King head		200.00-225.00
458. Battery set	circa 1915	100.00-120.00	Indian chief		250.00-275.00
Carbon filament light		5.00-7.00	Bottom: Howdy-Doody type		200.00-225.00
459. English set	circa 1915	275.00-325.00	Howdy-Doody type		175.00-200.00
460. Left: Carbon set (Propp)	about 1920	37.00-45.00	Pig		250.00-300.00
Right: Mazda set (Propp)	1920's	20.00-27.00	475. Left: Jester		80.00-90.00
461. Zelco set	1920's	100.00-125.00	Center: Dutch girl		50.00-60.00
462. Left Peerless set	1920's-1930's	18.00-22.00	Right: Snowman on skis		40.00-45.00
Right Santa Claus set	early 1930's	25.00-30.00	476. Top: Girl w/camera		40.00-45.00
463. NOMA candles set	1930's-1940's	40.00-50.00	Girl w/camera		27.00-35.00
464. Tree-top light	1920's-1930's	25.00-30.00	Girl w/a muff		25.00-30.00
465. Flourescent, boxed set	1940's	90.00-125.00	Baby in red dress		25.00-30.00
466. Flourescent, blue	1940's	30.00-35.00	Bottom: Aviator		25.00-28.00
all other colors	1940's	15.00-18.00	Boy		30.00-35.00
467. Common shape base		6.00-8.00	Baby in red sock		18.00-22.00
Rocket base		15.00-18.00	477. Top: Dick Tracy		75.00-95.00
468. Common shape base	1940's-1950's	6.00-8.00	Betty Boop		75.00-95.00
Oil filled lights		18.00-20.00	Little Orphan Annie		75.00-95.00
469. Krystal Star ea.		4.00-6.00	Moon Mullins		95.00-110.00
470. Large Matchless	1930's	50.00-65.00	Bottom: Andy Gump		95.00-110.00
Medium Matchless	1930's	20.00-25.00	Smitty		75.00-95.00
Small Matchless	1930's	10.00-15.00	Peewee		80.00-85.00
471. Top: Clown	circa 1910	40.00-50.00	478. Top: Girl head		25.00-30.00
Angel	circa 1910	30.00-35.00	Bottom: Kewpie doll		35.00-45.00
Cat with spectacles	1920's	60.00-75.00	Girl in a rose		35.00-45.00
Bottom: Snowman with club	circa 1910	25.00-28.00	Angel		25.00-35.00
Dwarf with shovel	circa 1910	55.00-60.00	Mrs. Claus		50.00-60.00
Horn player	circa 1910	60.00-65.00	479. Little Boy Blue		30.00-35.00
472. Large Father Christmas	circa 1915	85.00-95.00	Mother Goose		45.00-50.00

Plate No.	Date	Price
Humpty Dumpty bust		40.00-45.00
Humpty Dumpty		55.00-65.00
480. Three men in a tub		100.00-150.00
Clown		90.00-100.00
481. Top: Jackie Coogan		70.00-75.00
Canadian Mountie		100.00-125.00
Betty Boop		75.00-85.00
Bottom: Dog in clown suit		140.00-150.00
Flapper girl		50.00-60.00
Chinese schoolgirl		40.00-50.00
482. Top: Clown w/ruffled collar		25.00-30.00
Clown w/wide smile		35.00-45.00
Bottom: Clown w/ mask		28.00-30.00
Chubby clown		35.00-45.00
483. Common snowmen		15.00-22.00
484. Santa figure		20.00-25.00
Santa head		25.00-28.00
Santa scenes		35.00-40.00
485. Santa figures		25.00-40.00
Santa heads		20.00-35.00
486. Top: Hunchback Santa		20.00-25.00
Father Christmas		40.00-45.00
Mazda Santa		50.00-55.00
Bottom: Santa face on chimney		18.00-25.00
Standing Santa		18.00-20.00
487. Santa on a bell		15.00-18.00
Bottom: Left		15.00-18.00
Center		35.00-45.00
Right		35.00-45.00
488. Standing Santa		40.00-60.00
Santa head on a chimney		60.00-70.00
Tree-faced Santa		50.00-60.00
489. Top: Golfing rooster		28.00-35.00
Duck		28.00-30.00
Clown dog		35.00-38.00
Cat holding ball		80.00-85.00
Center: Dog in polo outfit		35.00-40.00
Chick		20.00-27.00
Horse in horseshoe		90.00-110.00
Bottom: Frog		18.00-25.00
Squirrel		40.00-50.00
Dismal Desmond		35.00-45.00
Mother cat & baby in basket		80.00-90.00
490. Top: Seated reindeer		45.00-50.00
Elephant		40.00-45.00
Bottom: Horseshoe		90.00-110.00
Pink panther		85.00-95.00
491. Top: Fish		20.00-25.00
Tadpole		40.00-50.00
Bottom: Dog on a ball		25.00-27.00
Pink elephant		25.00-35.00
Pig in a suit		50.00-65.00
Dog in a sock		75.00-85.00
Rabbit		35.00-45.00
492. Begging cat		30.00-40.00
Puffed-up cat		40.00-50.00
Cat with a banjo		18.00-25.00
Red seated Scotty		35.00-40.00
Two puppies in a shoe		100.00-150.00
Bulldog on a ball		30.00-35.00
493. Top: Dog with a baby		45.00-60.00
Owl with vest		40.00-50.00
Cat with apron		75.00-85.00
Hippo		90.00-110.00
Bottom: Round frog		200.00-250.00

Plate No.	Date	Price
Nesting dove		160.00-175.00
Pig with horn		80.00-90.00
Pig with drum		80.00-90.00
494. Top: Owl	1920's-1950's	55.00-65.00
Cat	1920's-1950's	30.00-35.00
Sitting dog	1920's-1950's	35.00-45.00
Wolf head	1920's-1950's	55.00-60.00
Bottom: Pink bear	1920's-1950's	115.00-125.00
Peacock	1920's-1950's	80.00-90.00
Burro	1920's-1950's	35.00-37.00
495. Top: Blue teddy bear		60.00-65.00
Bartender bulldog	1920's-1950's	80.00-90.00
Bear strumming banjo	1920's-1950's	20.00-25.00
Bottom: Kitten	1920's-1950's	40.00-50.00
Lion with tennis racquet	1920's-1950's	20.00-28.00
Cat in evening dress	1920's-1950's	100.00-115.00
Lion with pipe	1920's-1950's	45.00-50.00
496. Top: Cat	1920's	40.00-55.00
Lion	1920's	65.00-75.00
Owl	1920's	35.00-45.00
Monkey	1920's	45.00-55.00
Bottom: Birds	about 1900	18.00-22.00
Monkey	1920's	45.00-55.00
497. Common songbirds		18.00-22.00
498. Common parakeets		20.00-28.00
Miniature parrot		30.00-35.00
499. Cuckoo clock		20.00-28.00
House-shaped cage		25.00-30.00
Red birdcage		25.00-30.00
Yellow birdcage		20.00-25.00
500. Early bird		30.00-35.00
Peacock		50.00-60.00
Chick		30.00-35.00
Pelican		75.00-85.00
501. Common European birds	circa 1915	20.00-25.00
Larger European birds	circa 1915	35.00-40.00
502. European fruits	pre 1920's	30.00-45.00
European fruits	post 1920	15.00-20.00
503. Top: Pineapple		35.00-45.00
Grape cluster		20.00-22.00
Apple		20.00-25.00
Fruit cluster		20.00-22.00
Bottom: Grape cluster		20.00-25.00
Fruit basket		40.00-45.00
Grape cluster		20.00-25.00
504. Common flower		28.00-35.00
505. Flower in seashell		65.00-75.00
506. Rose		20.00-30.00
507. Seashell		30.00-35.00
508. Common house		15.00-18.00
509. Common lantern		5.00-12.00
510. Lantern	1920's-1930's	5.00-15.00
511. Common lantern		5.00-12.00
512. Hunter		30.00-32.00
Santa at the door		30.00-35.00
Santa in a sleigh		30.00-32.00
513. Star		20.00-25.00
Lantern		10.00-15.00
Ball with stars		20.00-25.00
Ball with holly		20.00-25.00
514. Zepplin		45.00-49.00
Ship		90.00-100.00
Tank		175.00-225.00
Auto		170.00-190.00
515. Silvered ornament		20.00-25.00

Plate No.	Date	Price		Plate No.	Date	Price
516. Top: Pink snowman	1930's-1950's	15.00-25.00				18.00-20.00
Dog on a ball	1930's-1950's	35.00-45.00		591. Nursery Rhyme Egg light	1930's	55.00-70.00
Parrot	1930's-1950's	30.00-35.00		520. Jack and Jill	1940's-1950's	225.00-250.00
Pink teddy bear	1930's-1950's	35.00-45.00		Old Lady in Shoe	1940's-1950's	125.00-150.00
Center: Indian head	1930's-1950's	90.00-110.00		Old Mother Hubbard	1940's-1950's	225.00-250.00
White snowman	1930's-1950's	12.00-15.00		Little Jack Horner	1940's-1950's	125.00-150.00
Kewpie	1930's-1950's	30.00-35.00		Mother Goose	1940's-1950's	75.00-85.00
Santa	1930's-1950's	18.00-20.00		521. Disney light		25.00-35.00
Bottom: Hound dog	1930's-1950's	65.00-85.00		522. Disney light		18.00-20.00
Santa head	1930's-1950's	15.00-20.00		boxed set		100.00-150.00
Bulldog	1930's-1950's	20.00-28.00		523. NOMA Mickey Mouse	late 1930's	100.00-150.00
Rabbit with walking stick	1930's-1950's	80.00-90.00		shades, set		
517. Top: Flower	1930's-1950's	20.00-30.00		524. Popeye Cheers set	early 1930's	100.00-150.00
Beach ball	1930's-1950's	20.00-30.00		525. Revolving shades set	late 1930's	40.00-45.00
House	1930's-1950's	20.00-25.00		526. Cardboard house	1930's	10.00-12.00
Center: Drum	1930's-1950's	25.00-35.00		527. Santa	1920's-1930's	40.00-45.00
Grapes	1930's-1950's	18.00-20.00		Dog	1920's-1930's	60.00-95.00
Lantern	1930's-1950's	12.00-15.00		Rose	1920's-1930's	30.00-33.00
Bottom: Auto	1930's-1950's	70.00-90.00		Cat	1920's-1930's	60.00-75.00
Lantern	1930's-1950's	12.00-15.00		528. GE prototype		70.00-75.00
Grape (clear)		20.00-25.00		529. Mirostar light		8.00-10.00
518. Miniature shapes		10.00-12.00		boxed set		60.00-70.00

Tree Stands

The highest priced and most desirable tree stands are the early musical ones. Some of the pre 1900 cast iron stands, which are very large and ornate, are also bringing excellent prices. The concrete stand with the Santa head is very desirable too.

Plate No.	Price		Plate No.	Price
530. Wind-up musical stand	270.00-300.00		534. Concrete with Santa head	200.00-225.00
531. Square cast iron stand	40.00-50.00		535. Concrete lighted stand	45.00-55.00
Musical stand for feather tree	75.00-100.00		536. Tin 3-ftd lighted stand	30.00-35.00
532. Wind-up musical stand	250.00-275.00		537. Metal rotator stand	25.00-35.00
533. Stand with Nativity scene	150.00-175.00			

Fences

Fences have been used around the base of Christmas trees for over one hundred years. The selling price of a fence will be determined primarily by the type of material from which it is made, and its age and condition. Cast iron, goose-feather, and wicker fences are very popular and are selling for the highest prices. Ornate tin fences and wooden fences made from hardwoods such as walnut are not far behind in price. The red and green wooden fences are more numerous and many can still be found at very reasonable prices.

Figure No.	Size	Price		Figure No.	Size	Price
538. Boxed goose-feather fence		550.00-600.00		546. Log fence	66" diamond	75.00-85.00
539. Goose-feather fence	20" x 20"	450.00-550.00		547. White wooden fence	20" x 20"	50.00-60.00
540. Wicker fence	24" x 24"	100.00-125.00		548. Tin fence, red and green	22" x 44"	100.00-120.00
541. Walnut fence	30" x 30"	160.00-180.00		549. Wooden fence, red and green	18" x 18"	25.00-30.00
542. Wooden fence, green & white	19" x 36"	85.00-110.00		550. Wooden fence, red and green	18" x 18"	45.00-55.00
543. Wooden fence		85.00-110.00		551. Wooden fence, red and green	18" x 18"	60.00-75.00
544. Lighted fence	92" octogon	125.00-150.00		522. Wooden fence, red and green		45.00-55.00
545. Wooden fence	44" x 66"	75.00-90.00				

Nativity Scenes – Villages – Animals

Many of the pieces of older nativity sets have been lost, and complete sets are hard to find. New sets are still being made of wood, plaster, paper, plastic, and other materials. Some of these newer sets are expensive when they are brand new, but they seldom bring their original price on the resale market.

German village pieces will usually command a slightly higher price than equivalent Japanese pieces. The older more elaborate village sets are more desirable.

Cotton, papier-mache, lead, and pewter animals are all being gathered up for use in Christmas settings. German animals from the early 1900's are attracting the most attention.

Plate No.	Price	Plate No.	Price
553. Nativity set	90.00-150.00	563. Sheep, Germany	60.00-65.00
554. Nativity set	50.00-75.00	564. White sheep, Germany	30.00-35.00
555. Nativity set	25.00-35.00	Black sheep, Germany	40.00-45.00
556. Building, large	30.00-35.00	565. Boxed set, sheep with shep-	125.00-150.00
557. Building, Japan	15.00-20.00	herd and dog	
558. Building, Japan	15.00-18.00	566. Spotted sheep, Germany	45.00-50.00
Building, Germany	18.00-25.00	567. Reindeer	10.00-12.00
559. Building, Japan	6.00-9.00	Sleigh	18.00-20.00
560. Building, Japan	8.00-12.00	568. Reindeer, papier-mache	25.00-35.00
561. Building, wood	20.00-25.00	Cardboard sleigh, Germany	10.00-15.00
562. Building w/ball decoration	8.00-12.00	569. Reindeer, metal	20.00-25.00

Bisque Figures

A variety of miniature bisque figures will be found. These pieces were made primarily in Germany, Japan, Czechoslavakia, and the United States during the 1920's and 1930's. The better detailed figures, usually German, will command the higher prices.

Plate No.	Size	Country	Price	Plate No.	Size	Country	Price
570. Bisque doll	4"		60.00-65.00	Snow baby waving	3¼"	Japan	20.00-25.00
571. Baby	1½"	Germany	85.00-100.00	578. Santa figures	2 – 3"		50.00-55.00
Bear	1¾"	Germany	40.00-45.00	Santa on bear	3½"		75.00-85.00
572. Jointed snow baby	3½"	Germany	200.00-225.00	579. Santa on sled	3"		40.00-55.00
Snow babies in red	2½"	Germany	75.00-95.00	Santa with reindeer	3¼"		50.00-75.00
573. Snow babies in blue	2½"	Germany	200.00-225.00	Santa with horse	2¾"	Germany	45.00-60.00
574. Planter	4½"		155.00-165.00	580. Miniature Santa	1½" – 3"	Germany	50.00-65.00
575. Snow baby on sled	2½"	Germany	45.00-55.00	Miniature Santa	1½" – 3"	Japan	40.00-50.00
576. Snowman	1¼"	Japan	45.00-55.00	581. Left	2½"		70.00-80.00
Snow baby	1¼"	Germany	60.00-75.00	Right	3"		70.00-80.00
Babies and slide	2"	Germany	155.00-175.00	582. Left	6"		65.00-85.00
Bear	1¼"	Germany	65.00-75.00	Right	3¼"		85.00-100.00
577. Snow baby on ball	3¼"	Japan	20.00-25.00	583. Left	2¼"		95.00-110.00
Seated snow baby	1¼"	Japan	20.00-25.00	Right	3½"		45.00-55.00
Snow bear	2"	Japan	30.00-40.00	584. Ring holder	3½"		15.00-20.00
Snow baby on sled	2¼"	Japan	20.00-25.00	585. Elf candleholder		Germany	35.00-40.00
Snow baby on skis	3⅓"	Japan	20.00-25.00	Elf candleholder		Japan	20.00-25.00

Candy Tins and Candy Containers

Prices for cake tins and candy containers have been climbing. The older Japanese and German candy containers are especially desirable and are rapidly disappearing from the marketplace. Expect the German papier-mache Santa figures to have the highest prices. In the past cake tins have been collected primarily for the signifance of their advertising. However, their popularity among collectors of Christmas decorations is increasing.

For Santa figural candy containers and their prices see the chapter on Santa figures.

Plate No.	Size	Country	Price	Plate No.	Date	Country	Price
586. Complete set	5" – 6"	Germany	250.00-300.00	Santa at chimney	3½"		50.00-60.00
587. Baby in shoe	4"		50.00-65.00	593. Roly-poly Santa	6"		400.00-500.00
Santa in chimney	4"	Japan	40.00-55.00	594. Santa w/pack			45.00-50.00
Drum	2¾"		25.00-28.00	595. Santa w/mesh bag			40.00-45.00
Corn husk nut cup	2¾"		25.00-30.00	Santa on bear			40.00-45.00
Santa on building	4"	Japan	40.00-55.00	596. Foil cornucopia	6"		35.00-40.00
Santa on sled	4"	Japan	40.00-55.00	597. Boot, left	6"	Japan	75.00-85.00
588. Chenille boot	4"	Japan	40.00-55.00	Boot, right	7"	Japan	95.00-120.00
Net bag	7"	Japan	85.00-95.00	598. Boot, left			25.00-30.00
Standing Santa	7"	Japan	95.00-110.00	Boot, left center			25.00-35.00
Wicker basket	4"	Japan	75.00-85.00	Boot, right center			85.00-90.00
589. Chenille basket	4"	Japan	85.00-100.00	Boot, right			90.00-100.00
Foil boot	6"	Japan	60.00-80.00	599. Snowman	9"	Germany	50.00-70.00
Net bag	7"	Japan	85.00-100.00	600. Snowman	5"		35.00-40.00
590. Boot	7"	Japan	90.00-100.00	Santa by ball	3¾"	W. Germany	35.00-45.00
592. Basket, green	4"	Japan	100.00-125.00	601. Snowman	6"	Germany	35.00-45.00
593. Horn w/Santa	4"	Japan	40.00-45.00	602. Santa	7"	Japan	85.00-95.00
Santa mesh bag	6"	Japan	90.00-100.00	Santa	9"	England	150.00-175.00

Plate No.	Size	Country	Price	Plate No.	Size	Country	Price
Snowman	7"	Japan	25.00-35.00	Stetson box	4"		45.00-50.00
603. Left	7"	Japan	35.00-40.00	610. Large tins	8 – 10"		45.00-55.00
Right	13"	Germany	45.00-60.00	Small tins	4 – 5"		40.00-50.00
604. Feather tree	6"		95.00-110.00	Rectangular tin	5" x 8"		45.00-55.00
605. House	6"		20.00-25.00	611. Rountree Cocoa			40.00-45.00
606. Santa in chimney			60.00-80.00	Jacob's Biscuits			40.00-45.00
Santa on rocking horse			60.00-80.00	Blue Bird Toffee			40.00-45.00
607. Santa box, left	10½"		15.00-20.00	CWS Biscuits			35.00-40.00
Santa box, right	10¾"		10.00-15.00	Carol Honor Candy			30.00-35.00
608. Santa face	4"		10.00-12.00	Huntley and Palmer			30.00-35.00
Cardboard box			3.50-5.00	612. Handled tin			45.00-50.00
609. Cardboard box			20.00-22.00	Small tin, oval			25.00-30.00
Heart	5"		20.00-22.00	613. Madison candy box			18.00-22.00
Small tins			40.00-45.00				

Chromos – Die-Cuts – Scraps

Old colorful chromolithographs have become very collectible. Santa Claus figures are the most popular. Large prints made before 1900, which are suitable for framing, are bringing the highest prices. Prints which remain in their original sheets are desirable.

Some reproductions of die-cuts are being sold. These copies lack the fine detail and the deep embossing of the originals. Also, most of the new ones are printed on thin stock. Some may be trimmed with tinsel or decorated with glitter.

Plate No.	Size	Price	Plate No.	Size	Price
614. Santa, red, top left	3¼"	5.00-7.00	618. Santa, red robe	9"	25.00-30.00
Santa, red, btm right	6¾"	7.00-9.00	Santa, blue robe	9"	25.00-30.00
Santa, red, btm left	6½"	6.00-8.00	Santa, green robe	9"	25.00-30.00
Santa, red	1½"	4.00-6.00	619. Santa in frame	10½"	60.00-70.00
Santa, white	6¼"	12.00-15.00	Santa head	3½"	5.00-6.00
Santa, white	1¾"	4.00-6.00	Santa head	6"	10.00-12.00
Santa, blue coat	4½"	10.00-12.00	620. Santa, left	12"	120.00-140.00
Santa head	1½"	3.00-5.00	Santa, right	6½"	45.00-55.00
Tree	4½"	6.00-8.00	621.	9½"	130.00-155.00
615. Santa, red, top left	4½"	7.00-9.00	622.	15"	130.00-160.00
Santa, gold coat, top left	4"	10.00-12.00	623.	12"	100.00-120.00
Santa, red	2"	3.50-5.00	624. Large figure	7"	30.00-35.00
Santa, red	4½"	5.00-7.00	Small figure	2"	3.50-5.00
Santa, red	6½"	7.00-9.00	625.	12"	100.00-120.00
Santa, white	3¾"	8.00-9.00	626.		35.00-40.00
Santa, blue	2"	4.00-5.50	627. Left	14"	30.00-35.00
Santa head	1½"	3.00-5.00	Right	9½"	25.00-35.00
Santa head	¾"	3.00-4.00	628.	14" x 22"	120.00-130.00
Tree	2½"	5.00-7.00	629.	11"	55.00-65.00
616. Santa torso, red	5½"	8.00-10.00	630.	16" x 10"	120.00-140.00
Santa torso & boots, red	4"	5.00-7.00	631.	21"	25.00-35.00
Santa torso & boots, blue	6"	10.00-12.00	632.	14"	25.00-30.00
Santa, gold robe	5¾"	12.00-15.00	633. Santa	10" x 6"	25.00-30.00
Santa, brown robe	5½"	12.00-15.00	Santa in sleigh	7" x 9"	35.00-40.00
Santa, red	2"	3.50-5.00	634.	10" x 6"	25.00-28.00
Children scene	5"	10.00-12.00	Santa in sleigh	7" x 9"	30.00-35.00
617. Santa, red robe	1¼"	3.00-4.50	635.		12.00-15.00
Santa, blue robe	1¼"	3.00-4.50	636.		18.00-20.00
Full sheet		120.00-150.00	637.		7.00-9.00

Christmas Prints

Plate No.	Size	Price	Plate No.	Size	Price
638. "Christmas Comes But Once a Year"	18" x 36"	95.00-125.00	Maud Humphrey		
			642. Maud Humphrey print	8" x 10"	65.00-75.00
639. Girl with puppies	18" x 22"	55.00-65.00	643. Little girl with red bonnet, Maud Humphrey	8" x 10"	75.00-85.00
640. "His First Christmas"		55.00-70.00			
641. "Four Seasons Calendar,"		75.00-85.00	644. Little girls with stocking,	11" x 14"	125.00-150.00

Plate No.	Size	Price	Plate No.	Size	Price
Maud Humphrey			by Marie Cornelissen		
645. "London Illustrated News" cover, 1893	13" x 18"	75.00-85.00	647. Stove pipe cover	dia 7"	60.00-70.00
			648. Tapestry	9" x 19"	100.00-125.00
646. "My New Bonnet"	11½" x 15"	100.00-125.00			

Prints From Children's Christmas Books

Plates 649 to 654

Prints taken from children's books normally sell for between twenty-five and fifty dollars. The more expensive ones are those of larger size which exhibit the fine detail of early lithography. Prints featuring Santa Claus and those with exceptional color will be in the higher end of this range. Also, those prints which can be attributed to a famous artist will bring higher prices.

Books

Many favorite children's stories have been reprinted numerous times by various publishers. Prices on books tend to vary greatly with age, condition, and subject matter. The material on which the book is printed and the number of color pictures included will also influence the price. If the book is illustrated by a famous artist, its value will be greater. There are a great number of old children's Christmas books still available, and prices are usually fairly reasonable.

Plate No.	Price	Plate No.	Price
655. The Night Before Christmas		659. Dennison's Christmas Book	
McLouglin Brothers, 1896	35.00-40.00	Catalog from Dennison Stores	15.00-20.00
656. Prints from the above book	25.00-30.00	Santa's Book	
657. Holly and Mistletoe		Eureka Stores	15.00-18.00
Belford Clark & Co.	25.00-30.00	660. Christmas Time in Action	10.00-15.00
Jolly Santa Claus		661. Santa Claus and the Lost Kitten	
Charles E. Graham & Co.	25.00-30.00	Whitman Publishing, 1952	15.00-18.00
The Robin's Christmas Eve		Santa Claus	
McLouglin Brothers	20.00-22.00	Whitman Publishing, 1947	15.00-18.00
The Night Before Christmas		662. Santa's Tuney Toy	
M.A. Donahue & Co.	30.00-35.00	Polygraphic Co. of America	20.00-25.00
658. A Gift From St. Nicholas		Santa's Circus	
McLouglin Brothers	25.00-30.00	White Plains Greeting Card Co., 1952	10.00-12.00
The Night Before Christmas and Other		663. Visions of St. Nick in Action	
Happy Rhymes From Childhood	20.00-25.00	Philips Publishers, Inc., 1950	10.00-12.00

Postcards

Collectors of Christmas postcards are competing with collectors of postcards in general for items in this category. Fortunately, in most cases there are plenty of cards to satisfy the demand, and the prices have remained reasonable. Many postcards are available for under ten dollars. The most heavily collected cards are those which were produced before World War I. Postcards with scenes signed by famous artists are attracting more attention, and their prices are gradually increasing. Two of the more popular artists are Frances Brundage and Ellen Clapsaddle. Postcards featuring a black Santa Claus are not often found. Other desirable cards are those which reveal a hidden scene when they are held to a strong light. Cards such as these and some of the other rarer cards may cost in excess of one hundred dollars.

Plate No.	Price	Plate No.	Price
664. Top left	12.00-15.00	Bottom right	7.00-9.00
Top right	7.00-8.00	667. Top left	12.00-15.00
Bottom left	12.00-15.00	Top right	12.00-15.00
Bottom right	12.00-15.00	Bottom left	12.00-15.00
665. Top left	22.00-27.00	Bottom right	12.00-15.00
Top right	22.00-27.00	668. Top left	12.00-15.00
Bottom left	16.00-18.00	Top right	12.00-15.00
Bottom right	20.00-22.00	Bottom left	10.00-12.00
666. Top left	10.00-12.00	Bottom right	8.00-10.00
Top right	5.00-7.00	669. Top left	7.00-9.00
Bottom left	10.00-12.00	Top right	10.00-12.00

Plate No.	Price	Plate No.	Price
Bottom left	10.00-12.00	Top right	8.00-10.00
Bottom right	7.00-8.00	Bottom left	16.00-18.00
670. Top left	10.00-12.00	Bottom right	6.00-8.00
Top right	8.00-10.00	677. Top left	10.00-12.00
Bottom left	6.00-7.00	Top right	9.00-11.00
Bottom right	25.00-27.00	Bottom left	9.00-11.00
671. Top left	5.00-7.00	Bottom right	6.00-8.00
Top right	7.00-9.00	678. Top left	10.00-12.00
Bottom left	7.00-9.00	Top right	8.00-10.00
Bottom right	6.00-8.00	Bottom left	8.00-10.00
672. Top left	20.00-22.00	Bottom right	10.00-12.00
Top right	10.00-12.00	679. Top left	6.00-8.00
Bottom left	8.00-10.00	Top right	6.00-8.00
Bottom right	8.00-10.00	Bottom left	6.00-8.00
673. Top left	12.00-15.00	Bottom right	6.00-8.00
Top right	6.00-8.00	680. Top left	5.00-7.00
Bottom left	7.00-9.00	Top right	5.00-7.00
Bottom right	12.00-15.00	Bottom left	5.00-7.00
674. Top left	7.00-9.00	Bottom right	5.00-7.00
Top right	6.00-8.00	681. Top left	16.00-20.00
Bottom left	10.00-12.00	Top right	10.00-12.00
Bottom right	8.00-10.00	Bottom left	6.00-8.00
675. Top left	6.00-8.00	Bottom right	7.00-9.00
Top right	5.00-7.00	682. Top left	7.00-9.00
Bottom left	6.00-8.00	Top right	7.00-9.00
Bottom right	10.00-12.00	Bottom right	6.00-8.00
676. Top left	10.00-12.00		

Trade Cards

Geographical location strongly influences the desirability and price of trade cards. Many collectors are seeking advertising memorabilia from their locality and will pay very high prices for items of local historical value. Thus, prices tend to vary significantly from one area to another.

In general, prices are usually moderate for cards produced after 1900. Earlier cards with quality printing are commanding the highest prices.

Plate No.	Advertiser	Date	Price	Plate No.	Advertiser	Date	Price
683. Left	Woolson Spice Co.	1890	30.00-35.00	Right	Woolson Spice Co.	early 1900's	16.00-20.00
Right	Woolson Spice Co.	1891	30.00-35.00	688. Left	Star Soap	early 1900's	20.00-22.00
685. Left	Woolson Spice Co.	1888	30.00-35.00	Center	Star Soap	early 1900's	20.00-22.00
Center	Woolson Spice Co.	early 1900's	16.00-20.00	Right	Star Soap	early 1900's	20.00-22.00
Right	Woolson Spice Co.	early 1900's	16.00-20.00	689. Left	M.E. DeVyer	early 1900's	25.00-30.00
687. Left	Woolson Spice Co.	early 1900's	16.00-20.00	Center	C.F. Ware Coffee Co.	early 1900's	25.00-30.00
Center	Woolson Spice Co.	early 1900's	16.00-20.00	Right	John F. Patton	early 1900's	25.00-30.00

Advertising

(Plates 691 to 706)

Generally, paper advertising from magazines is relatively inexpensive. A few exceptions are those choice ads which fall into a "double collectible" category where collectors from more than one area are seeking the ads, or exceptional ads with significant historical or political value. Such ads from older magazines – those dated prior to 1920 – are approaching twenty-five dollars in value.

Desirable ads from the 1920's and 1930's usually cost less than twenty dollars. Less desirable ads and ads from later dates can usually be found for under ten dollars.

Decorative Lamps

Santa figural lamps are attracting the most interest among collectors. They are the hardest to find and are the highest priced. Perhaps the most desirable Santa lamp is the U.S. Glass lamp shown in the first picture. Other older electric lamps are also very desirable. Those lamps which are least in demand are the newer plastic ones and the battery operated signal lamps.

Plate No.	Price		Plate No.	Price
707. Left	90.00-110.00		717. Santa w/brush trees	10.00-15.00
Center	800.00-1000.00		718. Rudolph	55.00-65.00
Right	150.00-200.00		719. Lamp	15.00-20.00
708. Left	50.00-60.00		Wreath	10.00-18.00
Right	150.00-200.00		720. NOMA auto light	50.00-55.00
709. Wreath	75.00-85.00		721. Wreath	40.00-55.00
710. Tree	40.00-45.00		Santa	30.00-45.00
711. Lantern	30.00-35.00		Snowman	40.00-60.00
712. Holiday bulb	40.00-60.00		Santa, right	30.00-35.00
713. Outdoor candle	20.00-22.00		722. Signal lamps, Santa	30.00-40.00
714. Santa bubble light	35.00-45.00		723. Left	10.00-12.00
715. Bubble lights	50.00-55.00		Right	8.00-10.00
716. Santa w/candles	25.00-30.00			

China and Glass

Good condition German china children's tea sets with Christmas decals are bringing premium prices. The supply is very limited and there seems to be no end to the demand. Prices are more reasonable for Christmas items from American potteries. There are a variety of nice cookie jars available for interested collectors. Some are not very old, but all are functional around Christmas.

Plate No.	Size	Country	Price	Plate No.	Size	Country	Price
724. Child's tea set	6-place	Germany	450.00-500.00	Creamer	2⅞"		25.00-30.00
Creamer	3"		30.00-35.00	Cup	2⅛"		18.00-20.00
Cup	2⅛"		22.00-25.00	Plate	5"		9.00-11.00
Plate	5⅛"		14.00-16.00	Saucer	4½"		5.00-6.00
Saucer	4½"		6.00-8.00	Sugar and lid	3⅝"		29.00-35.00
Sugar and lid	3"		35.00-38.00	Teapot and lid	4⅞"		100.00-125.00
Teapot and lid	5½"		125.00-150.00	731. Child's tea set	6-place	Germany	350.00-385.00
725. Child's tea set	6-place	Germany	360.00-450.00	Creamer	2⅞"		32.00-35.00
Creamer	3"		28.00-32.00	Cup	2⅛"		17.00-19.00
Cup	2⅜"		22.00-25.00	Plate	5"		8.00-10.00
Plate	7"		10.00-12.00	Saucer	4½"		4.00-5.00
Saucer	4¾"		5.00-6.00	Sugar and lid	3⅝"		35.00-37.00
Sugar and lid	3"		32.00-37.00	Teapot and lid	4⅞"		85.00-95.00
Teapot and lid	6½"		85.00-125.00	732. Merry Christmas			
726. Child's tea set	6-place	Germany	440.00-500.00	cup/saucer		Germany	25.00-30.00
Creamer	3¾"		30.00-35.00	733. Christmas scene			
Cup	2¼"		22.00-27.00	cup/saucer		Germany	30.00-40.00
Plate	5⅛"		14.00-16.00	734. Universal Pottery			
Saucer	4¼"		6.00-7.00	cup/saucer		America	12.00-18.00
Sugar and lid	4⅛"		35.00-40.00	735. Roseville Juve-		America	
Teapot and lid	6¼"		85.00-125.00	nile Set			
727. Child's tea set	6-place	Germany	450.00-500.00	Baby dish	7½"		150.00-200.00
Creamer	2¾"		35.00-37.00	Bowl	6"		150.00-200.00
Cup	2"		25.00-27.00	Creamer	3½"		125.00-150.00
Plate	4¾"		15.00-16.00	Cup/saucer			150.00-200.00
Saucer	3¾"		5.00-6.00	Plate	8"		175.00-210.00
Sugar and lid	3"		35.00-40.00	736. Watt creamer	4½"	America	150.00-200.00
Teapot and lid	5¼"		100.00-125.00	Watt custard	2½"	America	75.00-100.00
728. Child's tea set	6-place	Germany	405.00-500.00	737. Hall cookie jar	8½"	America	150.00-200.00
Creamer	2¾"		30.00-35.00	Hall bowl	5"	America	20.00-25.00
Cup	2½"		22.00-25.00	738. Hall Christmas			
Plate	6"		10.00-12.00	decal			
Saucer	4½"		4.00-5.00	Bowl, oval			30.00-35.00
Sugar and lid	3½"		35.00-40.00	Creamer			18.00-20.00
Teapot and lid	5"		85.00-125.00	Cup			15.00-18.00
Waste bowl	3½"		40.00-45.00	Plate	7¼"		10.00-12.00
729. Child's tea set	6-place	Germany	335.00-400.00	Plate	10"		20.00-25.00
Creamer	2⅞"		25.00-27.00	Platter	15½"		30.00-35.00
Cup	2⅛"		18.00-20.00	Saucer			5.00-8.00
Plate	5¼"		8.00-10.00	Sugar			18.00-20.00
Saucer	4¼"		5.00-6.00	Teapot			100.00-145.00
Sugar and lid			28.00-32.00	739. Taylor, Smith &			
Teapot and lid	5¼"		100.00-125.00	Taylor Party Set			
730. Child's tea set	6-place	Germany	335.00-400.00	Cup			8.00-10.00

Plate No.	Size	Country	Price
Plate			10.00-12.00
Saucer			3.00-5.00
740. Southern Potteries dinnerware			35.00-45.00
Cup			35.00-45.00
Plate			45.00-50.00
Saucer			3.00-5.00
741. American Bisque Company beverage set			
Cup			10.00-12.00
Tankard			75.00-85.00
742. Left, cookie jar		America	50.00-60.00
Right, cookie jar		America	100.00-125.00
743. Lucky Santa teapot	7½"	England	85.00-110.00
744. Cream pitcher		England	1800.00-2000.00
745. Lady head planters			
Left rear: Napco, 1959		Japan	45.00-55.00

Plate No.	Size	Country	Price
Center rear: Lefton		Japan	35.00-45.00
Right rear: Napco, 1956		Japan	35.00-45.00
Left front: INARCO		Japan	20.00-25.00
Right front: INARCO		Japan	20.00-25.00
746. Lady head planter, left			50.00-60.00
Lady head planter, center			45.00-55.00
Lady head planter, right			50.00-60.00
747. Girl figure with packages, lg			30.00-35.00
Girl figure with packages, sm			20.00-25.00
748. Bowl	5½"	America	8.00-10.00
Tumbler	5"	America	35.00-40.00
749. Christmas tree			10.00-15.00
Santa Claus			3.50-8.00

Danish Christmas Silver

(Plates 750 to 753)

Although the price of silver has fluctuated wildly in recent years, the quality and beauty of the Michelson creations have insured that these works of art will not depreciate. Most of the silverware produced before 1960 is selling for between $150.00 and $200.00. Later issues appear to be ranging between $80.00 and $100.00 on the resale market.

Costume Jewelry

Plate No.	Price
754. Figural Santa pins	18.00-35.00
755. Santa head pins	15.00-30.00
756. Angel pins	15.00-25.00
757. Reindeer bust pins	20.00-25.00
758. Reindeer pins	16.00-25.00
759. Bell pins	15.00-25.00

Plate No.	Price
760. Holly pins	12.00-20.00
761. Boot and stocking pins	15.00-25.00
762. Candle pins	12.00-25.00
763. Wreath pins	10.00-22.00
764. Miscellaneous pins	12.00-20.00

Cake and Candy Molds

The recent trend toward primitive accents has created an increased interest in old chocolate and cake molds. Collectors are finding these items make both attractive and fashionable kitchen hangings. The prices of the older, more elaborate molds have been high and are creeping slowly upward. Common tin and aluminum molds can still be found for very reasonable prices.

Plate No.	Size	Price
765. Teddy bear mold	5½"	90.00-110.00
Santa Claus mold	8"	95.00-125.00
Santa Claus mold	9"	100.00-130.00
766. Santa mold, tin	3"	20.00-25.00
Griswold mold	12"	150.00-200.00

Plate No.	Size	Price
Santa mold	4½"	40.00-45.00
767. Nordic-Ware mold	11½"	20.00-25.00
768. Tree mold	9"	15.00-18.00
Reindeer	3"	12.00-15.00
Santa cake pan	9"	10.00-12.00

Miscellaneous Prices

Plate No.	Price
769. Utility box	40.00-50.00
770. Fairbanks Soap box	200.00-250.00
771. Cotton stocking	175.00-195.00
773. Plaster Santa mold	150.00-200.00

Plate No.	Price
774. Father Christmas pipe	150.00-170.00
775. Compostion doll	150.00-175.00
776. Bing record player	70.00-85.00

Books on Antiques and Collectibles

This is only a partial listing of the books on antiques that are available from Collector Books. All books are well illustrated and contain current values. Most of the following books are available from your local book seller, antique dealer, or public library. If you are unable to locate certain titles in your area, you may order by mail from COLLECTOR BOOKS, P.O. Box 3009, Paducah, KY 42002-3009. Customers with Visa or MasterCard may phone in orders from 8:00 – 4:00 CST, M – F – Toll Free 1-800-626-5420. Add $2.00 for postage for the first book ordered and $0.30 for each additional book. Include item number, title, and price when ordering. Allow 14 to 21 days for delivery.

BOOKS ON GLASS AND POTTERY

1810	American Art Glass, Shuman	$29.95
2016	Bedroom & Bathroom Glassware of the Depression Years	$19.95
1312	Blue & White Stoneware, McNerney	$9.95
1959	Blue Willow, 2nd Ed., Gaston	$14.95
3719	Coll. Glassware from the 40's, 50's, 60's, 2nd Ed., Florence	$19.95
3311	Collecting Yellow Ware – Id. & Value Gd., McAllister	$16.95
2352	Collector's Ency. of Akro Agate Glassware, Florence	$14.95
1373	Collector's Ency. of American Dinnerware, Cunningham	$24.95
2272	Collector's Ency. of California Pottery, Chipman	$24.95
3312	Collector's Ency. of Children's Dishes, Whitmyer	$19.95
2133	Collector's Ency. of Cookie Jars, Roerig	$24.95
3724	Collector's Ency. of Depression Glass, 11th Ed., Florence	$19.95
2209	Collector's Ency. of Fiesta, 7th Ed., Huxford	$19.95
1439	Collector's Ency. of Flow Blue China, Gaston	$19.95
1915	Collector's Ency. of Hall China, 2nd Ed., Whitmyer	$19.95
2334	Collector's Ency. of Majolica Pottery, Katz-Marks	$19.95
1358	Collector's Ency. of McCoy Pottery, Huxford	$19.95
3313	Collector's Ency. of Niloak, Gifford	$19.95
1039	Collector's Ency. of Nippon Porcelain I, Van Patten	$19.95
2089	Collector's Ency. of Nippon Porcelain II, Van Patten	$24.95
1665	Collector's Ency. of Nippon Porcelain III, Van Patten	$24.95
1447	Collector's Ency. of Noritake, 1st Series, Van Patten	$19.95
1034	Collector's Ency. of Roseville Pottery, Huxford	$19.95
1035	Collector's Ency. of Roseville Pottery, 2nd Ed., Huxford	$19.95
3314	Collector's Ency. of Van Briggle Art Pottery, Sasicki	$24.95
3433	Collector's Guide To Harker Pottery - U.S.A., Colbert	$17.95
2339	Collector's Guide to Shawnee Pottery, Vanderbilt	$19.95
1425	Cookie Jars, Westfall	$9.95
3440	Cookie Jars, Book II, Westfall	$19.95
2275	Czechoslovakian Glass & Collectibles, Barta	$16.95
3315	Elegant Glassware of the Depression Era, 5th Ed., Florence	$19.95
3318	Glass Animals of the Depression Era, Garmon & Spencer	$19.95
2024	Kitchen Glassware of the Depression Years, 4th Ed., Florence	$19.95
3322	Pocket Guide to Depression Glass, 8th Ed., Florence	$9.95
1670	Red Wing Collectibles, DePasquale	$9.95
1440	Red Wing Stoneware, DePasquale	$9.95
1958	So. Potteries Blue Ridge Dinnerware, 3rd Ed., Newbound	$14.95
3739	Standard Carnival Glass, 4th Ed., Edwards	$24.95
1848	Very Rare Glassware of the Depression Years, Florence	$24.95
2140	Very Rare Glassware of the Depression Years, Second Series	$24.95
3326	Very Rare Glassware of the Depression Years, Third Series	$24.95
3327	Watt Pottery – Identification & Value Guide, Morris	$19.95
2224	World of Salt Shakers, 2nd Ed., Lechner	$24.95

BOOKS ON DOLLS & TOYS

2079	Barbie Fashion, Vol. 1, 1959-1967, Eames	$24.95
3310	Black Dolls – 1820 - 1991 – Id. & Value Guide, Perkins	$17.95
1514	Character Toys & Collectibles, 1st Series, Longest	$19.95
1750	Character Toys & Collectibles, 2nd Series, Longest	$19.95
1529	Collector's Ency. of Barbie Dolls, DeWein	$19.95
2338	Collector's Ency. of Disneyana, Longest & Stern	$24.95
3441	Madame Alexander Price Guide #18, Smith	$9.95
1540	Modern Toys, 1930 - 1980, Baker	$19.95
3442	Patricia Smith's Doll Values – Antique to Modern, 9th ed	$12.95
1886	Stern's Guide to Disney	$14.95

2139	Stern's Guide to Disney, 2nd Series	$14.95
1513	Teddy Bears & Steiff Animals, Mandel	$9.95
1817	Teddy Bears & Steiff Animals, 2nd Series, Mandel	$19.95
2084	Teddy Bears, Annalees & Steiff Animals, 3rd Series, Mandel	$19.95
2028	Toys, Antique & Collectible, Longest	$14.95
1808	Wonder of Barbie, Manos	$9.95
1430	World of Barbie Dolls, Manos	$9.95

OTHER COLLECTIBLES

1457	American Oak Furniture, McNerney	$9.95
2269	Antique Brass & Copper, Gaston	$16.95
2333	Antique & Collectible Marbles, 3rd Ed., Grist	$9.95
1712	Antique & Collectible Thimbles, Mathis	$19.95
1748	Antique Purses, Holiner	$19.95
1868	Antique Tools, Our American Heritage, McNerney	$9.95
1426	Arrowheads & Projectile Points, Hothem	$7.95
1278	Art Nouveau & Art Deco Jewelry, Baker	$9.95
1714	Black Collectibles, Gibbs	$19.95
1128	Bottle Pricing Guide, 3rd Ed., Cleveland	$7.95
1752	Christmas Ornaments, Johnston	$19.95
2132	Collector's Ency. of American Furniture, Vol. I, Swedberg	$24.95
2271	Collector's Ency. of American Furniture, Vol. II, Swedberg	$24.95
2018	Collector's Ency. of Granite Ware, Greguire	$24.95
3430	Coll. Ency. of Granite Ware, Book 2, Greguire	$24.95
2083	Collector's Ency. of Russel Wright Designs, Kerr	$19.95
2337	Collector's Guide to Decoys, Book II, Huxford	$16.95
2340	Collector's Guide to Easter Collectibles, Burnett	$16.95
1441	Collector's Guide to Post Cards, Wood	$9.95
2276	Decoys, Kangas	$24.95
1629	Doorstops – Id. & Values, Bertoia	$9.95
1716	Fifty Years of Fashion Jewelry, Baker	$19.95
3316	Flea Market Trader, 8th Ed., Huxford	$9.95
3317	Florence's Standard Baseball Card Price Gd., 5th Ed.	$9.95
1755	Furniture of the Depression Era, Swedberg	$19.95
3436	Grist's Big Book of Marbles, Everett Grist	$19.95
2278	Grist's Machine Made & Contemporary Marbles	$9.95
1424	Hatpins & Hatpin Holders, Baker	$9.95
3319	Huxford's Collectible Advertising – Id. & Value Gd.	$17.95
3439	Huxford's Old Book Value Guide, 5th Ed.	$19.95
1181	100 Years of Collectible Jewelry, Baker	$9.95
2023	Keen Kutter Collectibles, 2nd Ed., Heuring	$14.95
2216	Kitchen Antiques – 1790 - 1940, McNerney	$14.95
3320	Modern Guns – Id. & Val. Gd., 9th Ed., Quertermous	$12.95
1965	Pine Furniture, Our American Heritage, McNerney	$14.95
3321	Ornamental & Figural Nutcrackers, Rittenhouse	$16.95
2026	Railroad Collectibles, 4th Ed., Baker	$14.95
1632	Salt & Pepper Shakers, Guarnaccia	$9.95
1888	Salt & Pepper Shakers II, Guarnaccia	$14.95
2220	Salt & Pepper Shakers III, Guarnaccia	$14.95
3443	Salt & Pepper Shakers IV, Guarnaccia	$18.95
3737	Schroeder's Antiques Price Guide, 12th Ed.	$12.95
2096	Silverplated Flatware, 4th Ed., Hagan	$14.95
3325	Standard Knife Collector's Guide, 2nd Ed., Stewart	$12.95
2348	20th Century Fashionable Plastic Jewelry, Baker	$19.95
3444	Wanted To Buy, 4th Ed.	$9.95

Schroeder's ANTIQUES Price Guide

. . . is the #1 best-selling antiques & collectibles value guide on the market today, and here's why . . .

8½ x 11, 608 Pages, $12.95

• *More than 300 advisors, well-known dealers, and top-notch collectors work together with our editors to bring you accurate information regarding pricing and identification.*

• *More than 45,000 items in almost 500 categories are listed along with hundreds of sharp original photos that illustrate not only the rare and unusual, but the common, popular collectibles as well.*

• *Each large close-up shot shows important details clearly. Every subject is represented with histories and background information, a feature not found in any of our competitors' publications.*

• *Our editors keep abreast of newly-developing trends, often adding several new categories a year as the need arises.*

If it merits the interest of today's collector, you'll find it in *Schroeder's*. And you can feel confident that the information we publish is up to date and accurate. Our advisors thoroughly check each category to spot inconsistencies, listings that may not be entirely reflective of market dealings, and lines too vague to be of merit. Only the best of the lot remains for publication.

Without doubt, you'll find
SCHROEDER'S ANTIQUES PRICE GUIDE
the only one to buy for
reliable information and values.

COLLECTOR BOOKS
A Division of Schroeder Publishing Co., Inc.